Yorùbá Names
(Over 60,000 with correct pronunciation & meanings.)

Àpèdáto Òkẹ́ Mẹta
Orúkọ Yorùbá

láti ọwọ́ọ
Òdùbáyọ̀ Pópóọlá Odùṣínà

Copyright © 1998 - Odùbáyọ̀ Pópóọlá Odùṣìnà
All rights reserved.
National Library of Nigeria Cataloguing in Publication Data
CR 3080. Y65   027   1998   929.496333
ISBN-13: 978-1475075427
ISBN-10: 1475075421

Table of Contents

Introduction 1

Àpèdáto Àwọn Orúkọ Yorùbá Pẹ̀lú Ògidì Ìtúmọ̀ 3

The Basics of Yorùbá Language Pronunciation 4

The case for the use of assimilated low-tone-mark
".", in writing some Yorùbá names. 8

Radio and Television Presenters – How to
pronounce Yorùbá names correctly. 12

    What to do 12

    Advantages of the procedure: 12

Child-Naming system in Yorùbá culture. 14

    Modern Oddities 16

    Pet-names 16

    Role-Model Names 17

Names of regular family divinities or totems as
subjects of Yorùbá sentence-names or noun-
phrase-names 18

Common predicates of Yorùbá sentence-names or
couplings of non-phrase Yorùbá names as
appropriate with the subjects. 22

Non-Divinity and Non-Totem Nouns as Subjects of
Yorùbá sentence-names (with common predicates) 63

Àmútọ̀runwá (Names Brought From Heaven) 81

Situationally Created Names (Bí-ígbàá-ti-rí orúkọ
Adásọmọ) 87

Pet names, Nicknames and Titles that have become
Surnames (Àwọn orúkọ Àlàbọrùn-tó-Dẹ̀wù) 126

Common Traditional Pet-Names Or Affectionate
Names (Female) 146

Common Traditional Pet-Names Or Affectionate
Names (Male) 149

Àbíkú (Born-To-Die-In-Infancy) Names 152

About The Author 161

Table of Index 162

Introduction

The Yorùbá built and ruled the Ọ̀yọ́ empire along the West Coast of Africa during most of the slave trade centuries. The language therefore is still spoken by millions of people in modern-day Western Nigeria, Benin Republic, the Republic of Togo, and some parts of Sierra Leone.

Part of the people's culture is to name a child a week after birth, (7 – 9 days really), and give the child a name that is so situationally meaningful, that one can envisage the circumstances that surround the child's birth, or any significant event that occurred in the family at the time of the birth.

However, the Yorùbá language is strictly tonal, and was completely oral before the advent of the missionaries in the nineteenth century. Though the missionaries created a written form of it to produce bibles in the language and promote literacy in it in primary school, it was a punishable offence for students to speak the language in secondary schools during colonial years (up to 1960, at least).

One result of the prohibition is that present day Yorùbá speak the English language more, and understand it better than their Yorùbá language. Because they are not conscious of the 'sanctity' of the tones in the language, many of them pronounce Yorùbá names (including even their own) wrongly, and do not bother to know about the responsibilities of 'proper' behavior that the names put on them.

This book is an attempt to create the awareness of the significance of correct pronunciations of Yorùbá personal names, in the present and future generations of the people.

The essence of the book therefore, is to take Yorùbá people at home, and Yorùbá descendants in 'diaspora' back to the basics of cultural psyche and behavior of justice, reliability and valour, as contained in most of their traditionally REAL names (names given at 'christening;). Such names are expected to demonstrate the truism in the Yorùbá saying of:

1) Ilé là á wò kí a tó sọmọ lórúkọ, (we always look at the home/family situation before giving a name to a child), and

2) Orúkọ á máa roni, àpèjà á máa rònìyàn, (a person's name or family name motivates, even a pet-name shows in a person's character).

In addition, the major motivation for writing this catalogue of common Yorùbá names with the meanings of the names written in English, is to enlighten people with reference to the following:

a) At present, many Yorùbá people are not actively conscious of the fact that their names have meanings that are family/situation-specific, as to the circumstances of their births and expected befitting behavior.

b) The surnames of very many Yorùbá people nowadays were NOT peoples' names traditionally. They were names of military titles, social chieftaincy titles, etc., as well as nicknames.

c) Numerous Yorùbá names are so wrongly pronounced by Yorùbá people (including the bearer of the names) that the intended meaning of the givers of the names, during the naming ceremony (christening), is lost.

d) Even professional mass-media experts in Yorùbá language, who read news or read out advertisements in Yorùbá language on radio and television often pronounce Yorùbá names incorrectly.

e) Almost all Yorùbá, who have western education from secondary level to university, speak and write better English than Yorùbá. So, if the meanings of Yorùbá names are written in English, it will be easy for them to pronounce the names correctly, with the intended meanings, as well as name their own children meaningfully.

f) Many African-Americans in U.S.A., as well as descendants of Yorùbá in Brazil (Nàgó people), Haiti, Jamaica, and so on, have the wish to give Yorùbá names to their children. But they do not do so now, because they are not sure of how to do it intelligently, in consonance with situational meanings of family circumstances, at the time of the child's birth.

This book gives such Yorùbá descendants in diaspora, an avenue of intelligent selection of appropriate names for their children and grandchildren.

Àpèdáto Àwọn Orúkọ Yorùbá Pẹ̀lú Ògidì Ìtúmọ̀

Ó jó mi lọ́wọ́
Mo fi jó ẹnu,
Ó ta mí ní kìjí,
Mo yára ṣawo ìjímèrè,
Bí a ò pàjí hànjí, ẹrù kò níí ba ìjímèrè
Má-jẹ́ẹ́-á-gbọ́ ni, pé ọmọọ Yoòbá,
Kò leè pe orúkọ Yoòbá ní àpèdáto
Já gaara pẹ̀lú ògidì ìtúmọ̀.
Nìṣó ńlẹ̀, jẹ́ n kọ́kọ́ ta ọ́ lọ́fà ọ̀rọ̀
Kúmòólú lọ̀rọ̀ àgbà (ikú kò mú Olú, Olú kú, Olú kù)
Kì íṣe Kúmólú!!!
Lákòótan, oun tí ó fa kíkọ ìwé kékeré yí nípa àwọn orúkọ Yoòbá, àti kíkọ ìtúmọ̀ wọn ní èdè gẹ̀ẹ́sì ni pe:

1. Ọ̀pọ̀lọ́pọ̀ ọmọ Yoòbá kò mà pé orúkọ wọn ní ìtúmọ̀ tí ó ní 'torí' ni ẹbíi wọ́n nígbá tí a bí wọn.
2. Ọ̀pọ̀lọ́pọ̀ orúkọ Yoòbá ní òde òní ni kì í ṣe orúkọ gidi tẹ́lẹ̀tẹ́lẹ̀. 'Àlàbọrùn-tó-dẹ̀wù' ni wọ́n, nítorí orúkọ oyè ogun, oyè ẹgbẹ́, oyè èsìn, tàbí orúkọ àdájẹ́, àpèjà, àtẹ̀pè, tabi oríkì ni wọ́n tẹ́lẹ̀tẹ́lẹ̀.
3. Ọ̀gọ̀ọ̀rọ̀ àwọn orúkọ Yoòbá ni àwọn ọmọ Yoòbá pàápàá máa ń ṣì pè, débi pé wọn kò wá ní ìtúmọ̀ 'àárọ̀' (ní-ọjọ́-tí-a-fi-wọ́n-sọmọ) létí mọ́.
4. Àwọn ọ̀jọ̀gbọ́n ní èdè Yorùbá pàápàá, tí wọ́n ń ka ìròyìn, tàbí tí wọn ń ṣe ìkéde, àti ìpolówó ọjà ní éde Yorùbá láti inúu rédíò àti tẹlifísọ̀n, màa ń ṣi àwọn orúkọ Yorùbá pè. Bí àpẹẹrẹ, Apániṣílè ti di Apanisílé, Akíntilọ ti di Akíntilọ, Olúkolú sì di Olúkólú.
Ẹnìkan tilẹ̀ pe Àbẹrìgìdí ni Abẹ́rígidi!!!
5. Ó fẹ́rẹ́ jẹ́ gbogbo ọmọ Yoòbá tó mọ̀ọ́ kà láti ilé-ìwé girama lọ sókè, ni èdè gẹ̀ẹ́sì yé ju èdè Yorùbá lọ. Nítorí náa, tí a bá kọ ìtúmọ̀ àwọn orúkọ Yoòbá ní èdè gẹ̀ẹ́sì, yóò rọrùn fún wọn láti pe àwọn orúkọ náà ní àpèdáto pẹ̀lú ògidì ìtúmọ̀.
6. Ọ̀gọ̀ọ̀rọ̀ àwọn ìran mọ̀lẹ́bí Yoòbá tí wọ́n wà ní ilẹ̀ Amẹ́ríkà, Brazil, Hàìtì àti bẹ́ẹ̀ bẹ́ẹ̀ lọ ni wọ́n ń fẹ́ bu orúkọ Yorùbá sọmọ, ṣùgbọ́n tí wọn kò le ṣe bẹ́ẹ̀, nítorí wọn kò mọ bí wọ́n ṣe lè lo àwọn orúkọ tí yóò fi mọ́gbọ́n dání, láti fi hàn pé wọ́n mọ itúmọ̀ àwọn gbólóùn Yorùbá yìí pé:
    a. "Ilé là á wò kí a tó sọmọ lórúkọ"; ati "Orúkọ á máa roni, àpèjà á maa ròníyàn. Bí kò bá nídìí, obìnrin kì í jẹ́ Kúmòólú".
    b. Ìwé yìí fún irúfẹ́ àwọn ènìyàn bẹ́ẹ̀ ní àǹfààní láti yan orúkọ tó gbámúṣẹ́ fún àwọn ọmọ àti ọmọ-ọmọọ wọn.

Ire o.

The Basics of Yorùbá Language Pronunciation

Yorùbá is one of the easiest languages to pronounce its words because:

1) It is strictly a tonal language, in that the tones with which vowels in a word are pronounced, determine the meaning of the word. And there are only three (3), yes, only three tones – low tone, middle tone, and high tone.

2) The twenty-five letters of its alphabet comprise:
   a) eighteen consonants which all sound like the letters of the English alphabet except three (3) gb, p and ṣ.

   The "ṣ" has the English "sh" sound, as in **sh**all, **sh**ort, **sh**ot.

   The sound of the "gb" is not in the English alphabet, while the Yorùbá "p" does not sound exactly the same as in English. It is heavier, The pronunciation of the Yorùbá "p" is started with open lips, unlike the English/European "p" that is started with closed lips.

   Correct pronunciations of both the "gb" and the "p" therefore, are best learned when heard from someone who knows how to pronounce them.

   b) Seven vowels, each of which has a constant sound (irrespective of tone) any time it occurs in any word. (Latin and Italian are almost like it in this respect).

A. The Alphabet
Aa, Bb, Dd, Ee, Ẹẹ, Ff, Gg, Gbgb, Hh, Ii, Jj, Kk, Ll, Mm, Nn, Oo, Ọọ, Pp, Rr, Ss, Ṣṣ, Tt, Uu Ww, Yy.

B. The vowels and their sounds:
a as the "a" in ass
e as the "a" in tale
ẹ as the "e" in pet
i as the "e" in peep
o as the "o" in pole
ọ as the "o" in lot
u as the "oo" in wool

Note however that:
- a) "m" and "n" are tone-marked as vowels except when "m" or "n" is at the beginning of a word, and when 'n' is at the end of a word, in which cases, they remain consonants.

- b) When "n" or "m" stands alone as a word, it is also treated as nasal vowel to be tone-marked.

C. The Consonants: When the consonants are pronounced one by one (like when a child is reciting the letters of the alphabet), each of them sounds with an "ee" ending like "Bee".

B as in Bee

D as in Deed

F as in Feed

G as in Geese

Gb does not exist in English alphabet. Look for somebody who knows how to pronounce it correctly for you to learn.

H as in Heed

J as in Jean

K as in Keen

L as in Lean

M as in Mean

N as in Need

P an open-lips "p" sound, does not exist in English Language.

R as in Read

S as in Seed

Ṣ as in **Sh**e

T as in Tea

W as in Weed

Y as in Yeast

D. The tones:

1) **Low tone:** This is ALWAYS indicated with a high-left-to-low-right mark or stroke on top of the vowel "\" like a very, very, short demand curve in economics.

   For each of the vowels, it creates a sound like "a" in admix, avow. If these words were Yorùbá words the letter "a" would be tone-marked as admix or avow, with low tone mark "\" on the letter "a".

2) **Middle tone:** There is no mark on top of the vowel. For each one of the vowels, it makes the vowel sound like the dictionary pronunciation of the "a" as in analgesic, antagonistic, or animadversion. If they were Yorùbá words, there would be no tone-marks on the letter "a".

3) **High tone:** This is indicated with a low-left-to-high-right stroke or mark on top of the vowel "/", like a very, very short supply curve in economics. For each of the vowels, it makes the vowel sound like the "a" in marry, Alice, tarry or alum. If these words were Yorùbá words, the letter "a" would be tone-marked as follows: márry, Álice, tárry, and álum.

E. Practice words (Low tone), pronounce out loud, please

Àṣà	=	custom
Ọ̀nà	=	roadway
Ìjà	=	fight
Ìdì	=	bundle
Ṣàṣà	=	few
Bèbè	=	waist coral beads
Bẹ̀bẹ̀	=	plead or beg

F. Practice words (Middle tone), pronounce out loud, please

Ẹmu	=	Palm wine
Omi	=	water
Ẹja	=	fish
Oorun	=	sleep (noun)
Ẹran	=	meat
Ọmọ	=	child
Aya	=	wife
Ọkọ	=	husband
Igi	=	wood
Irin	=	Iron
Iṣu	=	yam

G. Practice words (High tone), pronounce out loud, please

Ló	=	twist
Pátápátá	=	completely
Ṣékélé	=	briefly
Lóólό	=	recently
Dájúdájú	=	surely
Pósí	=	coffin
Kínníkínní	=	in detail

H. Practice words (combination of tones), pronounce out loud, but slowly at first, and then read through six times, reading faster each time.

Ìfẹ́	=	*low–high*	=	love
Ògá	=	*low–high*	=	boss
Ilé	=	*mid–high*	=	house
Ilé ńlá	=	*mid-high-high-high*	=	big house
Ìfẹ́làjà	=	*low-high-low-low*	=	love ended the quarrel
Ìyàwó	=	*low-low-high*	=	wife
Ọlọ́mọtọ́ba	=	*mid-high-mid-high-mid*	=	one who possesses children is as important as a king

Jẹ́ kí a jọ sọ̀rọ̀ òwò nítorí owó
high-high-mid-mid-low-low-low-low-high-mid-high-mid-high
Let us discuss commerce because of money

Mo rí owó gbà, mo fi ra ońjẹ tán
mid-high-mid-high-low-mid-mid-mid-mid-high-mid-high
I received some money, I used all to buy food.

KEY:
high = high tone, "/"
mid = middle tone and
low = low tone. "\"

The case for the use of assimilated low-tone-mark ".", in writing some Yorùbá names.

Yorùbá is strictly a tonal language. Therefore, a wrong tone-mark on a vowel, or the absence of a tone-mark always gives a different meaning to the word.

Yorùbá was also a strictly oral language before the advent of Christian missionaries in the nineteenth century. The missionaries did a yeoman's job to evolve an alphabet for it, from the English (and Latin) alphabet, in order to produce bibles in Yorùbá language. They created the tone-marks which are still in use with some modifications.

However, one of the multitudinous proverbs in the language is:

"a kìí mọ̀ọ́ gún, mọ̀ọ́ tẹ̀, kí iyán ewùrà máà nẹ́mọ"– "one can never be such a skilled yam-pounder, to produce a lump less pounded-yam with water-yam".

In like manner, some pronunciations that create aural smoothness and certainties of meanings (when rendered orally), create "lumps" of doubt in meanings when put in writing with the existing tone-mark system.

A few examples of such are:

Adémósùn	=	Adé mú osùn	=	The crown chooses the camwood of parenthood
Adémósùn	=	Adé mú òsùn	=	The crown chooses divination powder
Adéníyè	=	Adé ní iyè	=	The crown has thoughtful mind/memory
Adéníyè	=	Adé ní ìyè	=	The crown has salvation (saves)
Olújájì	=	Olú já ijì	=	God broke the shocking fright
Olújájì	=	Olú já ìjì	=	God stopped the storm/problems
Ògúndáre	=	Ògún dá ire	=	The deity of iron provides good things
Ògúndáre	=	Ògún dá àre	=	The deity of iron pronounces me innocent/justifies my stand in the conflict.

It was in an effort to remove such "lumps" like these, that Professor Ayọ̀ Bámgbóṣé ingeniously initiated the use of "." to indicate the unexpressed low tone, and he called it the "assimilated low-tone mark", to be used in written Yorùbá.

The Yorùbá Orthography Development Committee met and deliberated on the adoption of the mark, but finally turned it down in normal writings.

Nonetheless, its use in names can make differences crystal clear as follows:

Adémósùn	=	Adé mú osùn	=	The crown chooses the camwood of parenthood
Adémó.sùn	=	Adé mú òsùn	=	The crown chooses divination powder
Adéníyè	=	Adé ní iyè	=	The crown has thoughtful mind/memory
Adéní.yè	=	Adé ní ìyè	=	The crown has salvation (saves)
Olújájì	=	Olú já ijì	=	God broke the shocking fright
Olújá.jì	=	Olú já ìjì	=	God stopped the storm/problems
Ògúndáre	=	Ògún dá ire	=	The deity of iron provides good things
Ògúndá.re	=	Ògún dá àre	=	The deity of iron pronounces me innocent/justifies my stand in the conflict.

In addition, many sentences and/or names with intended negativity, are WRONGLY pronounced as POSITIVE, when written under the existing tonal-marks system. Examples are:

Akínhánmi	=	Akín kò hán mi	=	I am NOT short of warriors (male children)
Akínṣòwón	=	Akín kò ṣòwón	=	The brave is NOT scarce in the family
Ayépọlá	=	Ayé kò pa ọlá	=	The world (people) has NOT killed (my) honour.
Kúrunmí	=	Ikú kò run mí	=	Death has NOT wiped my family out.
Ògúnbẹ̀là	=	Ògún kò bẹ̀ láti là	=	The iron deity did NOT beg/plead before becoming prosperous.
Ògúnbẹ̀rù	=	Ògún kò bẹ̀rù	=	The iron deity is NOT afraid.

Ògúnnòwó = Ògún kò sọ owó nù = The iron deity did NOT lose investments.

Olúṣọtẹ̀ = Olú kò ṣe ọtẹ̀ = The king is NOT conspiratorial.

Omíṣànlọ = Omí kò ṣàn lọ = The river deity did NOT flow away from our family.

Ọṣiínòwó = Ọṣì kò sọ owó nù = Ọṣì did NOT lose his investments.

Every one of them is commonly written and pronounced as positive without the "NOT" being indicated. The assimilated low-tone mark gives a clear indication of the negativity, when the names are written as in the following examples in paired comparison:

Akínṣọ̀wọ́n = The brave are scarce in the family

Akín.ṣọ̀wọ́n = The brave are NOT scarce in the family.

Ayépọlá = The world (people) have destroyed (my) honour.

Ayé.pọlá = The world (people) have NOT destroyed (my) honour.

Omíṣànlọ = The river deity has flowed away.

Omí.ṣànlọ = The river deity has NOT flowed away.

Ògúnbẹ̀là = The deity of iron pleaded to be prosperous.

Ògún.bẹ̀là = The deity of iron did NOT plead to be prosperous.

Akínhánmi = I am short of warriors (male children).

Akín.hánmi = I am NOT short of warriors (male children).

Kúrunmí = Death has wiped my family out.

Kú.runmí = Death has NOT wiped my family out.

Ògúnnòwó = The deity of iron lost money invested on this child.

Ògún.nòwó = The deity of iron did NOT lose money investing in this child.

In conclusion, the case for the use of the assimilated low tone in some Yorùbá names is very compelling, in that it clearly indicates where a low tone has been "swallowed" in a name, either:

1. To indicate negativity, or
2. To clarify the issue, that it is not a middle tone that has been "swallowed".

The assimilated low tone mark (.) is therefore recommended for use as necessary, to minimize the "lumps" and enhance correct pronunciations of the Yorùbá names, with intended meanings. It is sparingly used in this book.

Radio and Television Presenters – How to pronounce Yorùbá names correctly.

What to do

1) Know the names (and CORRECT Pronunciation) of Yorùbá family divinities, totem, etc. that most commonly begin Yorùbá sentence-names as subjects of the sentences. There are only about fifty (50) of them (see pages 18 – 21).

2) ALWAYS glance through your news-scripts, or advertisement copies to identify Yorùbá names in them.

3) Use this book to know the correct pronunciation of any predicate from its English meaning "as intended", or as "probably intended", and really practice the pronunciation, most especially, if it is a negative as in Fáàgbàmígbé (the oracle did not forget me).

4) If the name is not started by any of the family objects of worship, find the name among the lists of the other five categories of Yorùbá names in this book, and really pronounce it CORRECTLY, as tone-marked, in line with the English meaning, BEFORE going on air EVERY TIME.

Advantages of the procedure:

1) Newscasters, advertisers, continuity announces on radio and television will know the correct pronunciation (and meaning) of every name they come across in their scripts and pronounce them accordingly.

2) Listeners, especially the younger generation, will understand the names, learn the correct pronunciation from radio and television, and pronounce the names correctly themselves in oral language use.

3) Publishers will save money, in that they will have less corrections and less proof reading research to do on manuscripts, since writers will write names with correct tone marks initially.

4) Yorùbá language teachers in institutions of formal learning will "tidy up" their own pronunciation.

5) Mass-media customers of paid announcements will receive better value for their money.

6) Subsequent generations of radio and television newscasters and continuity announcers, advertisers, actors and actresses will pronounce Yorùbá names correctly.

7) Mispronunciation leads to mis-spelling in print, and the perpetuation of errors—the procedure will reduce such perpetuation significantly.

Child-Naming system in Yorùbá culture.

In Yorùbá culture, a child is given names ceremoniously on the seventh day if it is female, and on the ninth day if it is male. Twins are named on the eighth day. The principal names are normally given by the "family father" (pater familias) of the child's father, or by the child's father. Other names are given by the child's mother and by relatives who give names by dropping money (when money was all cowries/coins) into the bowl of water provided for the purpose at the naming ceremony.

The principal name(s) is usually determined in on one of five ways:

1) the name of the family's divinity or totem as subject of the sentence, plus the "action" that the divinity or totem has done with the birth of the child, as predicate.

   For example:
   - Ògún -- divinity of iron
   - Fúnmi – gives me
   - Òṣún – divinity of the river with that name
   - Rẹ̀mí -- pampers me

   Names of common divinities and totems are on pages 18 – 21
   The common predicates are on pages 22 – 64.

   The **60,000 names** in this book are constituted by using the name of each of the 50 deities/Totems on pages 18-21 as the subject of a sentence-name, with at least one thousand two hundred (1,200) out of the one thousand four hundred and forty nine (1,449) predicates on pages 22-64 as appropriate. The other kinds of names are additional.

2) the noun of a social item like Ọmọ (Child), Ọlá (honour), or Ayọ̀ (joy) being the subject of the sentence, while the predicate can be any of those in (1) above like Túndé (comes again), Délé (reaches home with me). See pages 66-82.

3) A meaningful creation, to depict the unique or overbearing family incident or situation at the time of the child's birth. Examples are:
   - Ìfẹ́làjà – love resolves the quarrel

- ✓ Ewéjẹ́—herbs were efficacious
- ✓ Abéjidé – one who arrives with the rain (born probably during the first rainfall in the year)

Such creations are listed on pages 88 – 127.

4a) An unusual or rare way of presentation of birth, makes the child have an automatic name "brought from heaven" (àmútọ̀runwá).

Examples are:
- ✓ Ìgè -- for a child born feet first rather than head first
- ✓ Táyéwò – the first one to taste the world and be born first of a set of twins.
- ✓ Kẹ́yìndé – the one that came last in a set of twins
- ✓ Òjó – a male child born with the umbilical cord around his neck.
- ✓ Àìná -- a female child born with the umbilical cord around her neck.

4b) Another way of giving an àmútọ̀runwá name to a child is when the name was prescribed by the diviner, even before the child's pregnancy took place, for example Amósùn, Dọ̀pẹ̀mú. The list of such names is on pages 83 – 87.

5) An insulting, derisive, instructive, or death – negating name is often given to a child who is believed to be an àbíkú (born to die young). A member of a band of nymphs believed to get themselves born as a male or female child, only to die young at a time prescribed by the band, and agreed to by the child before birth, in order to make the parents sad – the nymphs are believed to take delight in such sadness and tears!!! Such names are Olètúbọ̀ (the thief has come again), Àṣádé (the hawk has come), or Kúkọ̀yí (death has rejected this). See a list of common àbíkú names on pages 154 – 162.

Modern Oddities

Since the colonial era however, when the nuclear family system of bearing names was imposed on the Yorùbá non-nuclear system, the military titles, social titles, nicknames and pet-names, have become real surnames of many Yorùbá families. Examples of these are Balógun (military chieftain), Apènà (a cult title), Àrẹ̀mọ (the title of a heir apparent), Arówólò (a person who always has money to spend), or Àjíkẹ́ (a person who is woken up in the morning to be pampered). Such names as Yorùbá elders will say are "mufflers that became suits" – "àlàbọrùn tó dẹ̀wù". A list of common ones is on pages 128 – 147.

Pet-names

These are names given to people by adults who have special respect or affection for them, and cannot culturally use, or would not want to see their christening names. They are given in one of five situations:

1) Mother to child

2) Grandmother to child

3) Wife to husband, before first child is born

4) Wife to every household child who had been born before she was married to her husband

5) household wives to the new wife, before her first child is born.

There are male and female pet-names. The names can be literally meaningless or be a meaningful descriptive phrase. Examples of male pet-names are Àkànbí, Àjàní and Alóngẹ́ . Examples of female pet-names are Àbẹ̀bí, Àníkẹ́ and Ìdí-Ìlẹ̀kẹ̀.

(see the list of common ones on pages 148 – 150)

Role-Model Names

Naming a child after a notable person outside the family was not part of Yorùbá culture because every child was expected to behave according to the family traits in his/her name.

Names of regular family divinities or totems as subjects of Yorùbá sentence-names or noun-phrase-names.

	Divinity or Totem	Meaning in English
1	Adé	Crown, or 'the one who arrives'
2	Akin	The brave warrior
3	Àṣẹ̀n	A variation of Ùsẹ̀n, the family totem in honour of an Ìjẹ̀bú-Ìgbó heir apparent, who was sacrificed to avert conquest of the town by enemies.
4	Awo	Membership of a secret cult
5	Àyàn	The totem of vocational drummers.
6	Eégún	The re-incarnated ancestor, (an item of worship) personified in the family masquerade during the annual festival
7	Erin	Elephant; the family totem of the Aláàfin.
8	Èṣù	A divinity that is the principal messenger of all divinities, as invoked for good or evil effects on beneficiaries or victims respectively. (It is not satan as Christians and Muslims believe)
9	Ewé	Leaf or herb. It is used to depict herbalism as totem of oracular or herbalist families.
10	Ẹfun	White native chalk – the insignia of the divinity of Òrìṣà-oko, as family totem at the beginning of the names of female children of its worshippers (see Ọ̀ṣọ́)
11	Ẹ̀kí	The totem of Ondo warrior families
12	Èṣọ́	See Ọ̀ṣọ́
13	Ifẹ̀	Family totem of descendants of the few families that migrated to Ìjẹ̀bú from Ilé-Ifẹ̀
14	Ìbí	Pedigree or ancestry

	Divinity or Totem	Meaning in English
15	Ìpín	Fate, or endowments from heaven.
16	Ìtá	Orò worshippers' divinity (see Orò)
17	Òbí	Pedigree or ancestry (among Ìjẹ̀bús).
18	Odù	Ifá corpus
19	Ògún	Divinity of iron, worshipped mainly by families of blacksmiths, hunters and mechanics, who often use it to begin the names of their children.
20	Òkè	Mountain; worshipped, often for the river that flows out from under it.
21	Okù	Cord of very expensive coral beads worn on the wrist by holders of high chieftaincy titles. Used to begin peoples' names at birth to indicate belonging to the family of the high social status. (Ìjẹ̀bú language)
22	Okùn	Literary Yorùbá spelling of Okù above.
23	Olú	Originally referring to the family of the paramount chief, it is being used nowadays as a contraction of Oluwa – the Lord God.
24	Omi	Water as totem of families that worship a local water divinity and use only cold water exclusively to wash, feed and cure diseases – no herbs!
25	Òòsà	A "shibboleth" variant of "Òòṣa"
26	Òòṣà	A contraction of Òrìṣà an unspecified family divinity
27	Orí	One's head, fate.
28	Òrìṣà	Family Divinity not named specifically
29	Orò	The instrument of the secret cult for curfews, to allow members perform unsavoury public duties, like burying unidentified corpses, executing condemned robbers, or singing songs to expose evil-doers.

	Divinity or Totem	Meaning in English
30	Oṣó	The wisdom deity, wizard or seer – the totem of worshippers of Òrìṣà-oko, put at the beginning of names of male children. (See Ẹfun)
31	Otù	The supreme Chieftaincy title for appeasers of Ìjẹ̀bú national Divinities, as well as appeasers of the king's head (fate).
32	Oyè	Chieftaincy title, used as totem as the beginning of the names of children from families of titled chiefs, and of royal families.
33	Ọba	The divinity of small pox.
34	Ọdẹ	The hunter. Totem of families of vocational hunters and warriors.
35	Òjà	Family totem of immigrants from Ìjámọ̀ (Ondo) to Ìjẹ̀bú.
36	Òjẹ̀	A worshipper of the Egúngún/Eégún cult
37	Ọnà	Craftsmanship; the totem for the families of wood carvers and brass smiths.
38	Ọpá	Sticks for hitting drums. Used as totem by families of makers of drums and drummers.
39	Ọpa	The group insignia worshipped by members of the secret cult for curfews, the Orò cult.
40	Òpẹ̀	The Ifá divination palm-tree.
41	Ọrà	The totem of major Ilé-Ifẹ̀ families.
42	Ọrẹ̀	Another name of Ọpa the insignia worshipped by members of Orò cult.
43	Òṣà	A dialect contraction of Òrìṣà
44	Ọsì	The totem of Ìjẹ̀bú royal families
45	Òṣọ́	The family totem of the worshippers of Ọbàtálá, the divinity of elegant grooming, craftsmanship and ornamentation. They are vocational needle-workers, cloth weavers, tailors and goldsmiths.

	Divinity or Totem	**Meaning in English**
46	Ọ̀sun	The name of the woman who was drowned in the river that now bears her name. She got deified as the divinity of the river, and is worshipped mainly in areas comprising the present Ọ̀sun State.
47	Ọta	The granite, indicating the hard fighting and irrepressible "injun" or spirit of warrior families.
48	Ọya	The name of the most beloved wife of Ṣàngó, she was believed to have drowned in the River Niger near a village called Irá, and the Yorùbá named the river with her name. Her worshippers often put her name at the beginning of their children's names.
49	Ṣàngó	An ancient Aláàfin who got deified as the powerful divinity of lightning (and thunder).
50	(Ù) Ṣẹ̀n	See Àṣẹ̀n

Some people have had the predicates of their names cut away for so many generations that they do not know what the predicates are. They just bear the names of the subjects (divinity or totem) as their full surnames. For example:
- ✓ Rev. Ẹ̀ṣọ́,
- ✓ Dr. Ògún,
- ✓ Chief. Odù,
- ✓ Mrs. Ọ̀sọ́,
- ✓ Justice Òkè,

and so on.

Common predicates of Yorùbá sentence-names or couplings of non-phrase Yorùbá names as appropriate with the subjects.

	Predicate	Meaning
1	adé	crown
2	àga	chair (supreme)
3	ale	the tough (hard)
4	alẹ́	evening or night
5	bá	with; shortened form of bámiró – stay with me
6	bà	shortened form of bàmẹ̀rù – frightens me
7	bààbi	did not meet evil
8	bàále	comes back home
9	bade	meets or joins with crown
10	bádéjọ	assemblies with crown
11	bádémọsí	builds more with the crown
12	bádéró	stays with the crown
13	bàjò	comes back from the journey
14	bádéwò	gives birth to crown to see if it is good
15	bádéwọ̀	resides with crown
16	bákin	meets the warrior
17	bámbí	helps me to give birth
18	bámbọ̀	comes back with me
19	bàmẹ̀rù	frightens me
20	bámgbọ́pàá	helps me carry the drum sticks
21	bámgbóṣé	helps me carry óṣé – the Ṣàngó rod
22	bámi	meets me
23	bámidélé	gets home with me
24	bámigbọ́lá	helps me carry honour
25	bámigbọ́là	helps me carry wealth
26	bámíjọ	assembles with me. Befits me.
27	bámílọ́wọ̀	reaches my hand
28	bámiró	stays with me
29	bámiṣé	helps me to achieve it
30	bámiṣígbìn	helps me open the ígbìn drum
31	bámitẹ́fá	helps me spread out Ifá or satisfy Ifá
32	bángbádé	helps me carry crown

	Predicate	Meaning		Predicate	Meaning
33	bángbálà	helps me carry, (wear) the white cloth of Òrìṣà-oko divinity	52	béjiró	stays with the rain
			53	béjìró	stays with the twins
			54	bẹ́kún	meets weeping
34	bángbé	lives with me	55	béyìnbó	gives birth to a very light skinned child (like a European)
35	bángbọ́lá	helps me carry honour			
36	bánibọrí	worships / appeases one's head			
			56	bẹ̀ẹ́kún	did not meet weeping
37	bángbọ́là	helps me carry wealth	57	.bẹ̀là	did not plead / beg to be rich / to survive
38	bánjí	wakes up with me			
39	bánjọ	assembles with me or befits me	58	bẹléwò	pays the house a visit
40	bánkalẹ̀	sits down with me	59	bẹ̀mẹ́kún	pleads with me to stop weeping
41	bánkẹ́	pets/pampers (child) with me	60	bẹ́nà	mixes with ornamentation
42	bánkọ́lé	builds house with me	61	.bẹ̀rù	is not afraid
43	bántálẹ́	stays with me till night (old age)	62	bẹ́ṣin	meets a horse (that can be used in warfare)
44	.banwí	did not scold / chastise me	63	bẹ́wàjí	wakes up with beauty (a female name)
45	bánwòó	looks after it (child) with me			
			64	bẹ́yẹmí	breathes with dignity
46	báre	meets goodness	65	bí	gives birth
47	barí	touches with head	66	bíba	gives birth to father
48	báwo	meets cult	67	bìínú	is not annoyed (with the family)
49	báyìíwá	comes with "this"			
50	báyọ̀	meets joy	68	bílé	gives birth to another child after the one before.
51	báyọ̀ńlé	meets joy in the family			

	Predicate	Meaning		Predicate	Meaning
69	bílẹ̀jẹ́	does not ruin the house	84	bógun	joins or meets up with the army
70	bímjọ	gives birth to many of "me" or to resemble an ancestor	85	bogun	comes back from war
71	bímpé	gives birth to me in complete health	86	bógunjókòó	stays or settles down with the army
72	bímtán	gives birth to me in good shape	87	bógunró	stays with the army
73	bíntán	language variant of bímtán above.	88	bógùn-ún-ró	stays with the divinity of iron - Ògún
74	bísáyé	is born into the world.	89	bójòwá	comes in with rain
75	bísáyè	gives birth to, in a proper place	90	bòkun	comes back from the ocean
76	bisẹ́yìn	did not draw back or recede.	91	bólú	meets Olú the paramount chief/king
77	bísí	gives birth to more	92	bólújókòó	stays with Olú the king
78	bísúgà	gives birth to more palaces (every prince is a palace)	93	bòmi	covers me, or crowns me
			94	bòmẹ́yìn	cover my back, supports
			95	borí	wins or succeeds
79	bíyàá	gives birth to mother	96	bórò	meets with oró festival
80	bíyè	gives birth to a survivor	97	bótù	meets otù or gives birth to otù, a high chieftaincy in Ìjẹ̀bú
81	bíyìí	gives birth to this, a child of the deity			
82	bódù	gives birth to Odù the Ifá corpus	98	bótùjọ	assembles with otù
			99	bòwá	overwhelms us
83	bódùdé	arrives with Odù	100	bóyè	meets the crown

	Predicate	Meaning		Predicate	Meaning
101	bóyèdé	arrives with the crown, chieftaincy title, or university graduation	118	bọ́ládé	arrives with honour
102	bóyèró	stays with the title	119	bọ́làdé	arrives with wealth
103	bọ̀	comes back	120	bọ́lájí	wakes up with honour
104	bọ̀ádé	comes back into crown	121	bọ́lánlé	meets honour at home
105	bọ́ba	meets the small pox	122	bọ́láòtán	child to be called Bọ́lá (meet honour) is not finished yet
106	bọ̀bókun	comes back to meet the sea / ocean, (affluence)	123	bọ́lápé	assembles with honour – other children
107	bọ̀bọ́lá	comes back to meet honour	124	bọ́lárìndé	walks in with honour
108	bọ̀bọ́yè	comes back to meet title	125	bọ́lárìnwá	See bọ́lárìndé
109	bọ̀de	comes back	126	bọ́látì	supports honour
110	bọ́dẹdé	comes back with the hunter	127	bọ́nà	meets ornamentation
111	bọ́dún	meets with festival	128	bọ́nàdé	arrives with craftsmanship
112	bọ́dúndé	arrives with the festival	129	bọ́ni	meets with a worthy person
113	bọdunrìn	walks (in) with the festival	130	bọ̀ọ́pọ̀	is restored
114	bọ́dúnpìtàn	narrates history with the festival	131	bọ́rọ̀	gives birth to wealth, or meets wealth
115	bọ́jẹ̀	gives birth to ancestor worshipper	132	bọ́rọ̀dé	arrives with wealth
116	bọ́lá	meets with honour, or gives birth to honour	133	bọ̀sí	returns to
			134	bọ̀sípò	returns to its position, is restored
117	bọ́là	meets wealth or gives birth to wealth	135	bọ́ṣìdé	arrives with Ọṣì (the king)

	Predicate	Meaning		Predicate	Meaning
136	bọ́ṣìró	stays with Ọṣì (the king)	153	búsìn	meets worship (of family divinity)
137	bọ́ṣọ̀ọ́ró	stays with Ọ̀ṣọ́ ornamentation	154	bùsíyì	adds to prestige
138	bọ́tẹ̀	meet with rebellion or war	155	bùsóyè	adds to title
			156	bùsọ́lá	adds to honour
139	.bọ́ùn	does not lament or give up	157	bùsúyì	adds to prestige
140	bọ̀wálé	comes back home	158	búṣẹ̀n	mixes with ùṣẹ̀n family, the totem name of ancient Ìjẹ̀bú princes
141	bọ́yaró	stays with Oya, the deity of River Niger	159	bùṣe	is not finished, is still functional
142	bùfúnmi	gives me part	160	buyì	gives prestige to me
143	bùgà	divides the palace (with the arrival of a new son)	161	dábirí	sees / chooses here specially
			162	dadé	becomes a crown
144	bùkọ́lá	adds to honour	163	dádé	wears a crown
145	bùkúnlé	adds to the house (family)	164	dáìíní	holds on to this
			165	dáìíró	keeps this alive
146	bùúlé	does not abuse or insult the house (family), upholds family honour	166	dákun	appeases
			167	dálùú	founds a town
			168	dámilọ́lá	honours me
147	búléjọ	assembles with the house / befits the house	169	dámipé	creates me in perfection
			170	dámitán	creates me perfect
148	búlùdé	arrives with drums	171	dàmọ́lá	mixes with honour
149	bùlújẹ́	does not spoil or ravage the town	172	dánà	creates the road
150	bùnmi	gives me as a gift	173	dàpọ̀	mixes with a family with the same divinity
151	bùsáyọ̀	adds to joy	174	dára	is good
152	bùsí	adds to, increases	175	dárà	performs wonders

	Predicate	Meaning		Predicate	Meaning
176	daramọ́lá	mixes with honour	199	déunmọ́lá	covers something in addition to honour in container
177	dáramọ́lá	is good in addition to having honour
178	daramódù	mixes with odù	200	dèyí	becomes "this"
179	dáre	justifies	201	dèyíbí	becomes "this" to be born
180	dàṣẹ	becomes the authority	202	dẹ̀jọ	becomes eight
181	dáùnsi	responds to it	203	dẹkẹ́	becomes a house pillar
182	dayọ̀	becomes joy
183	dé	arrives	204	dẹ́kọ̀ọ́	appeases
184	dèé	binds him/her	205	dẹ́kún	stops weeping
185	dégà	arrives at the palace	206	dẹ̀réyìnọ̀tá	eventually outlives the enemy
186	dèjì	becomes two
187	déjoyè	arrives to assume chieftaincy	207	dẹ̀rọ̀	becomes easy
208	dẹ̀rù	becomes an item of awe or fear
188	délé	arrives at home
189	délíni	arrives at our house (Oǹdó)	209	dẹtí	listens
210	dẹ̀yìn	becomes the backbone (support), comes back
190	delùú	arrives the town
191	délùúrẹ̀	arrives at his/her town	211	dẹ̀yìnbọ̀	comes back here
192	démi	covers my head
193	démiládé	cover my head with crown	212	dibú	becomes a large expanse of water
194	dèmurẹ̀n	becomes another one
195	délélà	gets home and becomes rich	213	digba	becomes two hundred (many)
196	dépò	reaches rightful position	214	dìgbòlú	collides with
215	diímú	holds on to this
197	dèrè	becomes a profit	216	diípọ̀	becomes many
217	dìjọ	becomes a congregation
198	dèrù	becomes an object of awe or fear

#	Predicate	Meaning
218	dìjí	becomes a noble, as a member of the Onígbẹ̀ẹ̀tì royal family
219	dìmákin	holds on to the brave (akin)
220	diméjì	becomes two
221	dìmímú	supports me or holds on to me
222	dínà	blocks the way of evil doers
223	dìínà	does not block the way
224	dìínàọlà	does not block the way to wealth
225	dínàọ̀tá	blocks the way of the enemy
226	dìọọ̀sẹ̀	arrives on a worship day
227	dípẹ̀	stops people's consolation by giving me joy
228	dipúpọ̀	becomes many
229	dìran	becomes hereditary
230	dire	becomes something good
231	direpọ̀	packages good things together
232	dìṣẹwọ́	takes as first blessing
233	dìtán	armours completely
234	dìtàn	becomes history
235	dìtí	becomes a heap
236	díyà	compensates for ill treatment

#	Predicate	Meaning
237	díyàn	stops famine (barrenness)
238	díyàolú	compensates olú for ill treatment / punishment
239	dìyímú	holds on to this
240	dó	settles / establishes a settlement
241	dodimú	holds on to the fort
242	dogun	becomes an army (protection)
243	dógunró	stops the army
244	dòójútìmí	does not shame me
245	doku	becomes strength (Ìjẹ̀bú)
246	dòku	becomes the ocean (Ìjẹ̀bú)
247	dokun	becomes strength
248	dòkun	becomes the ocean
249	dolíẹ̀	becomes a possessor or builds his house (Oǹdó)
250	dolú	becomes paramount
251	dósẹkún	settles to stop weeping
252	dòsùmú	holds on to Ifá divine staff
253	dóṣù	appoints a month

	Predicate	Meaning
254	doṣù	becomes the moon (a thing of joy to see)
255	dó.ṣù	creates an island of human population
256	dótará	settles with relatives
257	dótẹbí	settles with family members
258	doyè	becomes chieftaincy
259	doyin	becomes honey
260	dojà	becomes a market
261	dọlápọ̀	mixes honour together
262	.dọ́nàgbọ́	does not hear about it (the birth) on a journey
263	dọpẹ́	thanks or becomes gratitude
264	dosùn	becomes parenthood (camwood paste)
265	dọrọ̀	becomes wealth
266	dọta	becomes granite (unconquerable)
267	dòtun	becomes new
268	dubù	becomes a vast expanse of water
269	dúgbà	keeps its appointed time

	Predicate	Meaning
270	dugba	becomes two hundred (many)
271	dugbèé	is not possible to be lifted, has become awesome
272	dúgbèé	is not possible to lift (possess) it
273	dùn	is sweet
274	dùnjoyè	is sweeter than title
275	dùnmóyè	is sweet in addition to chieftaincy
276	dùnmọ́mi	pleases me
277	dùntán	is completely sweet without blemish
278	dù-ún-bá-rin	is profitable / sweet to be associated with
279	dùn-ún-sìn	is profitable to worship
280	dúrógan	stands solidly by (me)
281	dúrógo	stands solidly by (me)
282	dùúyìgbé	does not allow loss of prestige
283	dúyìlé	increases prestige
284	dúyìíle	lets this (family) increase
285	ewu	danger
286	éyingbó	does not praise the forest; survives

	Predicate	Meaning		Predicate	Meaning
287	éyùn- ún-gbó	does not go into the forest; survives	305	farakàn	touches with body; espouses
288	èkọ́	learning or education	306	farasin	hides self humbly
289	èsan	compensation	307	faratì	rests itself (here)
290	ẹ̀ẹ̀tàn	does not deceive	308	farayíọlá	adorns body with honour
291	fadé	draws crown	309	farayọ́lá	contraction of above farayíọlá
292	fadébọ̀	draws crown to come back	310	fáyé	loves the world
293	fadéjù	is superior with the possession of the crown	311	fèsì	replies (with this child)
294	fadékẹ́	pampers with the crown	312	féyìdé	wants this to come
295	fadẹ́kẹ́mi	pampers me with the crown	313	fèyíkẹ́	pampers with this
296	fadérìn	uses the (prestige of) crown to walk with pride	314	fèyíkẹ́mi	pampers me with this
			315	fèyímí	breathes with this
297	fadérògbà	uses the crown to encircle in support	316	fẹ̀intọ́lá	rests its back on honour
			317	fẹ̀jọ́	quashes the case / quarrel
298	fadéṣeré	plays with the crown	318	fẹ̀kọ́	expands learning
299	fajó	brings about dancing	319	fẹlá	expands honour
300	fàlà	draws the white cloth of the deity near	320	fẹlé	expands the house
			321	félẹ́yẹ	loves the dignified person
301	falú	draws olú	322	fẹ́mi	loves me
302	fàlú	draws the town (people) together	323	fẹ́milójú	takes care of me
303	farajímákin	moves with the brave	324	fẹ̀inwó	see fẹ̀yinwó
304	fará	pulls relatives (near)			

	Predicate	Meaning
325	fẹ́miwá	loves me enough to come and find me
326	fẹ́nòjọ	loves craftsmanship
327	fẹ̀sọ̀	expands /uses carefulness
328	fẹ́sọ̀	loves carefulness
329	fẹ̀sọ̀bí	gives birth to, carefully
330	fẹ́wa	loves us
331	fẹ́yiídé	loves this to come
332	fẹ́yìnmi	wants me to be praised
333	fẹ̀yintọ́lá	rests its back on honour
334	fẹ̀yìnwó	mothers the child completely with piggy-backing
335	fì	is great, is large
336	fiadé	mixes with or puts into the crown
337	fìjàbí	gives birth to with a fight or quarrel
338	fimíhàn	points me out
339	fiolú	mixes with or puts into an Olú family
340	fìranyè	survives through the attributes of pedigree
341	fisan	compensates with
342	fisáyọ̀	adds to joy
343	fìwàbí	gives birth to with (good) character
344	fiyèbí	gives birth to through thoughtful understanding
345	fiyèsí	pays attention to
346	fólú	loves olú
347	folúkẹ́	pets with olú
348	folúṣọ́	watches or protects with God
349	fónyèkẹ́	gives oyè (title) to pet
350	fọ̀sílẹ̀	exhibits itself
351	foṣùdó	born on the day of new moon or establishes with the moon
352	fowóbí	gives birth to with money
353	fowódè	ties it down (ensure its survival) with money
354	fowókẹ́	pampers with money
355	fowópè	calls with money
356	fowórà	buys with money
357	fóyèkẹ́	gives title (oyè) to pamper
358	fọdúnrẹ̀n	walks in during the annual festival (Ìjẹ̀bú)

#	Predicate	Meaning
359	fọdúnrin	the Yorùbá spelling of fọdúnrẹ̀n
360	fọ́lá	loves honour
361	fọlábí	gives birth with honour
362	fọlábọ̀	pulls honour back home, or comes back with honour
363	fọládé	pulls honour to arrive, or arrives with honour
364	fọlágbadé	receives the crown in grand style
365	fọlájì	gives me honour (Oǹdó/Ìjẹ̀bú)
366	fọlájìn	gives me honour
367	fọlájù	exceeds others in honour
368	fọláké̩	pampers with honour
369	fọlámí	breathes with honour
370	fọláràn	extends honour (to many)
371	fọlárin	walks with honour
372	fọláṣadé	makes honour its crown
373	fọláwiyọ́	washes hand with honour as water
374	fọláwún	bluffs with honour
375	fọláyími	rubs me with honour
376	fọre	speaks good tidings
377	fọ́soyè	disperses / mixes up with chieftaincy
378	fọ́ọ̀tẹ̀	does not love / support rebellion / conspiracy
379	fọwọ́kàn	reaches or touches with hand
380	fọwọ́tẹ̀	creates settlement singlehandedly
381	fùjàmádé	captures / takes the crown with a fight
382	fulẹ̀	arrives - Ìjẹ̀bú
383	fúnmiláyọ̀	gives me joy
384	fúnmikẹ́	gives me to pamper
385	fúnmiládé	gives me a crown
386	fúnmilókun	gives me stamina / strength
387	fúnmilọ́lá	gives me honour
388	fúnmilọ́pẹ́dá	gives me cause to be grateful
389	fúnnbí	gives me to give birth to
390	fúnndé	gives me to arrive here
391	fúnnṣọ́	gives me to watch over
392	fúnnwá	gives me to arrive here
393	fúnwapé	gives us completely

	Predicate	Meaning		Predicate	Meaning
394	fùrẹ̀n	makes the walk worth it - Ìjẹ̀bú	412	gorúwà	supreme in all manners of living
395	fùrìn	makes the walk worth it	413	goyè	ascends the chieftaincy
396	fusan	compensates with it	414	gún	is straight / upright
397	fuṣíkà	uses it to fulfil promise	415	gúnà	straightens the road, is right
398	fùsì	extols fame	416	gúndoyè	walks tall, waiting for the chieftaincy title
399	fùwà	extols or compensates (good) character	417	gúnjú	has a fine face
400	fuwá	becomes or fits us	418	gúnlẹ̀	arrives
401	fùwàpé	behaves with complete magnanimity	419	gúnlóyè	is comfortable in the chieftaincy seat
402	fùyè	creates survival / salvation	420	gúnnà	straightens the road
403	fuyì	creates dignity	421	gùnlọlá	climbs into honour
404	gadé	climbs unto the crown	422	gúnwà	sits on the throne
405	gẹbọ̀	comes back majestically	423	gúwà	the Ìjẹ̀bú variant of gúnwà
406	gẹyè	assumes the title	424	gúnyè	establishes a chieftaincy title
407	gindí	establishes the root	425	gùbádé	climbs to meet the crown
408	gojù	too tall / strong	426	gbadé	accepts crown
409	gòkè	climbs up	427	gbádé	picks up the crown
410	golú	is supreme, climbs to become paramount	428	gbádébọ̀	brings back the crown
411	gonáyà	is brave, is strong in chest	429	.gbàgbé	did not forget (its promise)
			430	gbàjà(jà)	takes the fight (against me) as its fight

	Predicate	Meaning		Predicate	Meaning
431	gbajú	commands attention	447	gbèjà	supports me in the conflict
432	gbàkẹ́	receives to pamper	448	gbélélà	becomes wealthy or survives, without leaving home
433	gbàmí	saves me			
434	.gbàmígbé	does not forget me			
435	gbàmílà	receives me to salvation, saves me	449	gbéléró	keeps the family going
			450	gbèmí	supports me
436	gbàmíyè	receives me to survive, saves me	451	gbéjúadé	brightens the face of the crown
437	gbáñmú	grabs me and holds on to me, to save me	452	gbèmílà	supports me to salvation
438	gbàrò	considers (my case), heard my supplication / invocation	453	gbémilékè	lifts me to be on top, makes me excel
			454	gbémiró	lifts me to survive
439	gbáròyé	listened to pleading	455	gbémisọ́lá	lifts me into honour
440	gbayì	receives prestige	456	gbenga	lifts me high
441	gbàyíbí	helps in the save delivery of this one	457	gbéñle	lifts me above (on top)
			458	gbéñró	contracted form of gbémiró
442	gbàyíbọ̀	receives and brings this back (home)	459	gbénúṣọlá	stays in the womb to enjoy (long overdue delivery)
443	gbàyílà	saves this one			
444	gbàyìn	receives praise (and blesses me)	460	gbéyìró	supports this prestige
445	gbè	supports	461	gbewésà	collected the herbs to administer healing
446	gbégbáajé	carries the calabash of investments; starts to be highly profitable	462	gbẹ́bẹ̀	accepts pleadings

	Predicate	Meaning		Predicate	Meaning
463	gbẹ̀dẹ̀lọ́lá	easy and generous in honour	479	.gboùngbé	does not forget its promise
464	gbẹ̀gì	populates the wasteland or receives the coral beads of kingship	480	gbóùnmi	heard my pleading
			481	gboyè	accepts or occupies the throne / chieftaincy title
465	gbẹ̀ìn	supports solidly, receives the back and back bone	482	gbọ́	heard (my pleading)
			483	gbọ̀dùn	received and considered my sadness and consoles me
466	gbẹ́kún	heard my weeping and consoles me			
			484	gbọlá	receives honour
467	gbẹ̀san	avenges (me)	485	gbọlà	receives wealth
468	gbẹ̀yẹ	receives dignity	486	gbọ́làgún	straightens wealth
469	gbilé	crowds the home	487	gbọ́n	is wise
470	gbilẹ̀	expands, crowds the land	488	gbọnà	receives ornamentation
471	gbìtẹ́	occupies the throne	489	.gbọ̀nmírè	did not pass me bye (without blessing me)
472	(i)gbó	forest, farmland			
473	gbòjà	settles the quarrel	490	gbọrọ̀	receives wealth
474	gbólúadé	takes the highest crown	491	gbọ́rọ̀	listened
			492	gbọ̀sẹ̀	accepts rituals of worship
475	gbólúwadé	mixes Olú with crown			
476	gbóríoyè	occupies the throne	493	gbọ́tibaba	accepts father's pleadings or advice
477	gborúwà	accepts the ultimate in character, accepts kingship or the throne	494	gbúlélà	becomes wealthy without leaving home
			495	gbùlú	expands, saves or occupies the town
478	gboṣó	accepts wisdom			

	Predicate	Meaning
496	.gbùlúgbé	does not forget the town, (continues to protect the town)
497	gbùre	receives blessings
498	gbùsẹ̀n	accepts rituals of worship
499	gbùsì	accepts popularity or being famous
500	gbùsìn	accepts rituals of worship
501	gbúsìn	hears being worshipped or is worth being worshipped
502	.gbùtí	does not accept being ridiculed
503	gbùwà	accepts or receives (character) rituals of worship
504	gbuyì	becomes prestigious
505	gbùyìn	is worth being praised, or accepts praise of worship
506	gbúyìró	sustains prestige
507	hánmi	is scarce for me
508	.hánmi	is not scarce for me
509	tilọ	did not walk away, or has not gone (away)

	Predicate	Meaning
510	ìpé	is not complete yet
511	ìtan	is not finished yet
512	ììtan	never finishes
513	ìyè	of salvation or of survival
514	ìpẹ̀	consolation
515	jádesọ́lá	comes out into honour
516	jagunlà	fights war to become rich
517	jájì	breaks the sudden fright/fear
518	já.jì	breaks the storm
519	jákàn-ń-dè	releases the captive
520	jáladé	barges / gate crashes into crown
521	jánà	is correct
522	jàre	is vindicated
523	jáyàn	ends the famine of childlessness or male births
524	jààyàn	does not end the famine
525	jáyìí	plucks this, give birth to this
526	jèéjí	did not steal
527	jẹ́	agrees, allows good occurrence
528	jẹ̀ẹ́	does not allow (evil occurrence)

#	Predicate	Meaning
529	.jẹ̀bi	is not guilty
530	jẹ́mbíyàá	allows me to give birth to mother
531	jẹ́mbíára	allows me to give birth as addition to my people
532	jẹ́mbíáyọ̀	allows me to give birth to more joy
533	jẹ́mbọ́là	allows me to meet wealth
534	.jẹmígbẹ́	does not cheat me
535	jẹ́miísìn	is easy for me to worship
536	jẹ́milẹ́yìn	allows me to have a back bone
537	jẹ́milúà	allows me to have a future
538	jẹ́milúsì	allows me to be famous
539	jẹ́miníyì	allows me to have prestige
540	jẹmirímú	allows me to see (a child) to catch / take (to be a parent)
541	jẹ́mirókùn	allows me to find beaded wrist band of honourable chieftaincy
542	jẹ́mirúwà	lets me enjoy prosperity
543	jẹ́ẹ́mitẹ́	does not let me lose respect
544	jẹ́mitó	allows me to measure up to expectations
545	jẹnrọ́lá	helps me to see honour
546	jẹñrọ́mọkẹ́	helps me to have children to pamper
547	.jẹ́ñtẹ́	does not let me lose respect
548	jẹ̀ẹ́ódúnmí	gives me relief, does not let the incident pain me
549	jẹ́ógbọ́	answers and listens
550	jẹ́pè	answers the call
551	jẹṣíkù	is prosperous
552	jíbíkẹ̀ẹ́	gives birth in the morning to someone to be pampered
553	jíbówú	wakes up to meet the black smith's mallet or gives birth in the morning to iron mallet (heir apparent to the blacksmith)
554	jíbóyè	gives birth in the morning to the title or wakes up to meet the title
555	jídé	arrives in the morning
556	.jígà	does not steal the palace
557	jíire	wakes up well/ healthy

	Predicate	Meaning
558	jìmí	gives or dashes me
559	jímibọ́lá	allows me to meet honour
560	jímirígbà	allows me to find to collect
561	.jímitẹ́	saves me from losing respect
562	jinlẹ̀	is deep (strong)
563	jìṅmí	gives or dashes me
564	.jinrí	is perfect, is not deformed
565	jìrẹ̀n	forgives the walk (wandering to other deities by the father, or going to another husband and back by the mother)
566	jírẹ̀n	walks/arrives early in the morning (Ìjẹ̀bú)
567	jírìn	same as jírẹ̀n
568	jìrìn	forgives the walk
569	jíwẹ̀	gets cleansed early in the morning
570	.jìyà	does not suffer
571	.jìyàgbé	did not suffer in vain
572	jíyan	wakes up and walks proudly
573	.jiyàn	agrees; did not argue

	Predicate	Meaning
574	jíyọ̀	wakes up to be jealous
575	jìíyùn	does not steal coral beads, merits it
576	jógbìn	dances the ìgbìn drum, is happy
577	jòógbìn	does not dance the ìgbìn drum because the child is disappointingly female
578	jòkun	is as expansive as the ocean
579	.jóùnbọ́	does not allow (me) to regret
580	.joùngbé	fulfills its promise
581	joyègbé	assumes the title irrevocably
582	.joyègbé	does not allow the title to be lost, or upholds the chieftaincy
583	joyètán	assumes the title irrevocably
584	jọ	assembles
585	jọbí	gives birth jointly
586	jọ̀bí	resembles pedigree
587	jọjú	is worthy of expectation, appreciable
588	jọkẹ́	pampers jointly
589	jọkún	has assembled plentifully
590	jọlá	enjoys honour

	Predicate	Meaning
591	jọláoṣó	enjoys the honour, or help of the wise (oṣó)
592	.jọ́lápamọ́	does not allow honour to be hidden
593	jọ́láyẹmí	lets honour fit me
594	jọlé	assembles the house (family)
595	jọ̀lú	assembles the town
596	jọmóyè	assembles/flocks around the chieftaincy
597	jọmpọ̀	two families of the same divinity or totem mix together
598	jọmọ	assembles children
599	.jọnyọ̀mí	does not let them gloat over me
600	jọ́nwò	takes care jointly
601	jọọ́lá	assembles into honour
602	jọtán	has assembled completely or finished assembling
603	jọtó	has assembled enough
604	jọ̀wà	assembles (character) posterity
605	júbàá	is possible to approach appeal to
606	jùmọ̀	is better/more important than knowledge
607	jùmọ̀bí	gives birth together / jointly
608	jùmọ̀kẹ́	pampers jointly
609	jùsíbẹ̀	is still superior
610	júsìgbé	does not allow fame to be lost
611	jùwọ́n	is superior to them
612	juyì	is superior to prestige
613	júyìn	is worthy of being praised
614	jùúyìgbé	does not allow prestige to be lost
615	jùúyìtán	does not allow prestige to be finished
616	kàísí	reckons with this one
617	káláiwo	is famous, has noise
618	kalẹ̀	sits down, settles
619	kàmísí	reckons with me or recognizes me
620	kàn(mí)	reaches (me)
621	kanlè	reaches the house
622	kanlú	reaches / touches olú
623	kànmí	reaches me, touches me, is my turn

	Predicate	Meaning		Predicate	Meaning
624	kànmíbí	is my turn to give birth to	643	kìran	strengthen the lineage
625	kànóyè	signals or mixes with chieftaincy	644	kíyèsí	takes note of
626	kanlá	reaches honour	645	kò	arrives, emerges
627	kañyè	reaches title	646	kóìkí	publicizes
628	kányisádé	drops honey into crown	647	kòjẹ́	does not allow misfortune
629	kányisọ́lá	drops honey into honour	648	kójọ	assembles/ collects
630	káyọ̀dé	brings joy	649	kókun	fills the ocean (the house with children)
631	kẹfun	collects white chalk, mixes with Òrìṣà-oko worshipping family	650	kolú	meets and combines with honour (olú)
632	kẹmi	pampers me	651	kolùújọ	assembles the town
633	kẹmibí	pampers me to be a parent	652	kòmáyà	gives me courage
634	kẹnu	becomes popular, is on everyone's lips	653	kòtán	still remains
			654	kóredé	brings good fortune
635	kẹyẹ	has (collects) dignity	655	kówàdé	behaves to type positively
636	kidé	comes in boldly	656	kówàjọ	assembles (character)
637	kìígbé	does not waste away	657	kóyè	fills or collects titles
638	kilẹ̀dé	comes in marching loudly	658	kóyèdé	collects and brings titles
639	kimíláyà	assures me, gives me courage	659	kóyèjọ	assembles titles
			660	kóyindé	brings honey, happiness
640	kinládé	is bold on the throne or is a strong crown	661	kóyọ̀wá	collects and brings salt/ happiness
641	kinmíléyìn	supports me			
642	kira	is strong	662	kọlá	collects honour

Predicate		Meaning		Predicate		Meaning
663	kọ́ládé	collects and brings honour	680	kungà	fills the palace
664	kọ́lájọ	assembles honour	681	kúnlé	fills the house
			682	kúnmojú	is appreciated by me
665	kọ́láwọlé	collects and brings honour into the house	683	.kúòlíẹ̀	does not leave his house
666	kọ́lé	builds the house	684	kùótù	is still left (remaining) among the otú
667	kọ́gà	builds the palace			
668	kọ́rọ̀dé	brings in wealth	685	kùọ́wọ́	remains in hand, not finished
669	.kọtíikún	did not turn a deaf ear; listened	686	kùsíbẹ̀	is still there, still remains there
670	kọ̀yà	compensates ill treatment, fights one's cause	687	kùútán	did not all die
			688	kútì	did not all die
671	kù	remains (has not all died)	689	kutú	does wonders
672	kúàdé	assembles and brings posterity, behaves to type positively	690	kúwàdé	assembles and brings posterity/good character
			691	láàánú	is merciful
673	kúàjọ	assembles posterity	692	labí	is what we give birth to
674	.kúgbé	did not die in vain	693	labú	crosses a large expanse of water
675	kúkù	did not all die	694	ladé	is the crown
676	kùlẹ́yìn	there is more, remains behind	695	làdé	emerges safely
			696	ládùn	has sweetness
677	kúnbi	completes/ ends asking (for female child)	697	laè	opens the memory
			698	lagun	survives the war
678	kúnbí	are many here			
679	kúnbìí	adds to pedigree	699	láiwo	is noisy, famous (Òǹdó)

	Predicate	Meaning		Predicate	Meaning
700	làjà	settles the quarrel	717	laríwò	is what we see/find to take care of us
701	láki	has the brave (to give) (Ìjẹbú/Òndó)	718	.lákokò	is active all the time, does not have special time
702	lákin	has the brave (to give)			
703	lakin	is the brave	719	làrù	survives the fright
704	làkun	crosses the ocean, survives difficulties	720	làrùbọ̀	survives the fright and arrives safely
705	lakùn	opens and adorns the coral beads of honour	721	làsọ́dẹ	survives or opens into the hunter's family
			722	làsọ́pẹ́	opens into gratitude
706	làlú	makes the town prosperous	723	làsóyè	opens into chieftaincy
707	làmbọ	is the one we worship			
708	lámì	has a mark/milestone	724	.lásùnmú	does not need to be caught (approached), cunningly
709	làmíwá	is what we are looking for, searching for	725	làṣẹ	is the supreme
			726	láṣẹ	has supreme authority
710	lànà	constructs the road, creates the way	727	làtẹ̀	survives the rebellion/war
711	laní	is what we have (for help)	728	làwọ́n	diluted them (usually male child after many females)
712	lànbẹ̀	is the one we are begging			
713	lànkẹ́	is what we pamper/worship	729	láyà	is courageous
			730	layé	is life
714	lànwá	is what we are searching for	731	layè	opens the memory
715	larí	is what we see/find	732	láyọ̀	has joy
716	làrin	splits iron, does the impossible	733	layọ̀ọlá	is the joy of ọlá (honour)

	Predicate	Meaning
734	lé	increases
735	(i)lé	domestic
736	lèébìtà	does not have filth
737	lédùn	drives away sadness
738	lékan	increases by one
739	lèékútì	does not fail to drive death away
740	lemára	makes me well
741	.lemára	does not make things difficult for me
742	lémọ	increases the number of children
743	lénà	leads the way
744	lérù	is awesome (Èkìtì)
745	lésì	has a response
746	létí	has ears, listens
747	léwe	has children (to give people)
748	léyìímú	chased and caught this
749	.lẹ	is not lazy
750	lẹbọ	is the appropriate sacrifice
751	léègàn	has no reproach
752	lẹ́kàn	increases by one (Ìjẹ̀bú)
753	.lẹ́mọ	has no fault, is perfect

	Predicate	Meaning
754	lẹ́nu (ọ̀rọ̀)	can fulfill expectations, is capable
755	lẹ́rù	is awesome
756	lẹ́sẹ	has rows, does things in rows and in order
757	lẹ́sin	has (horses) for warfare
758	lẹ́.yẹ	has dignity
759	líjàdù	has to be scrambled for
760	líṣàbí	has to be selected for proper breeding
761	lí.yè	has salvation
762	líyè	has good memory
763	lóbíi	gives birth to it
764	lódèé	ties (the child) down
765	lódire	becomes good luck
766	lókìkí	is famous
767	lókò	is what it meets at home
768	lókun	has stamina
769	lókùn	has beaded wrist band of honour
770	lolù	is supreme
771	lóòótọ́	is honest
772	lótó	is the one (divinity) that is enough

	Predicate	Meaning
773	lóunpé	has everything completely, is perfect
774	.lọ	does not go, continues to support
775	lọdún	is the exceptional festival
776	lọlá	is honour
777	lóla	has a future
778	lọmí	dignifies me supremely
779	lóòsẹ̀	has a personal house/abode
780	lọ́pẹ́	is worthy of being thanked
781	.lọtán	did not all go; still remains
782	lọ́tẹ̀	evokes envy/hatred
783	lọ́wọ̀	has respect
784	lọwọ́kàn	is its turn, is the one touched next
785	.lu	did not leak
786	lù	mixes with
787	lùádé	mixes with crown
788	lùdé	beats a drum on arrival (cries extra loud)
789	.lúgbàgbé	does not forget
790	lúkọ̀yà	is the one who compensates one for being ill-treated
791	lùọlá	mixes with honour
792	lùsì	is fame
793	lúsì	has fame
794	lúsi	has investments/wealth
795	lùwọyè	drums/gate crashes into the throne, or chieftaincy
796	mádé	mixes with crown
797	mádégún	dignifies the crown
798	mágbagbéọ̀ọlá	does not forget honour
799	májẹ̀ẹ́ntẹ́	does not allow me to be ridiculed
800	mákin	mixes with the brave
801	mákindé	brings the brave
802	mákinwá	brings the brave
803	màláolú	knows and conforms with God's imagination for me
804	mámẹ̀	takes on the (birth) mark
805	máyàki	emboldens, encourages
806	máyọkún	makes joyful, brings maximum joy
807	máyọ̀wá	brings joy here
808	mejiwá	brings rain

	Predicate	Meaning
809	mérù	takes away fear (Èkìtì)
810	mèsì	knows the reply
811	mébùdé	brings multiple birth
812	mèwò	knows how to look after, or how to take care of
813	mẹ́fun	takes white chalk, mixes with chalk, the symbol of Òrìṣà-oko worshippers
814	mègbọ́n	knows and respects elders, knows the wise
815	mẹ́kàn	takes one, or takes its own turn
816	mẹ́rù	takes the fear away; eliminates fright
817	mẹ́sò	comes the easy way
818	mèṣọ́ọ́	dresses befittingly; knows ornamentation; is fashionable
819	mẹ́ṣọ̀ọ̀	prefers craftsmanship or ornamentation
820	midé	mine has arrived
821	mígòké	mine has increased
822	miíjù	mine is superior
823	míkanra	breathes to reach others, is in touch
824	mìílà	mine survives or is wealthy
825	miládé	mine has crown
826	milárá	mine has relatives
827	milẹ́gẹ́	mine is delicate
828	milékàn	mine increases by one
829	milókun	mine has stamina
830	milọ́ni	mine has relatives
831	milúyì	mine has prestige
832	mipé	mine is complete
833	mipéjú	mine is ever present
834	mísí	increases
835	mpé	contraction of mipé
836	mitóyè	mine is as valuable as a chieftaincy title
837	módù	joins with Odù
838	.mójúro	does not make me sad, does not dash my expectations
839	mókùn	mixes with coral bead (wrist bands)
840	mókun	becomes encouraged
841	mólú	mixes with Olù

#	Predicate	Meaning	#	Predicate	Meaning
842	moónáyàájọ́	mine has the ultimate power or voice of creation	858	mọ́dẹdé	brings in the hunter
			859	mọdi	builds the wall
843	moógòkè	mine has excelled	860	mọ́dún	chooses the time of the annual festival
844	móògùnjẹ́	lets medicine become efficacious	861	mọ́lá	mixes with honour or chooses honour
845	moore	is grateful			
846	moríyọ́	makes me joyful at sighting it	862	mọ̀la	knows tomorrow, is all-seeing
847	morótì	is the one that I live (abide) with	863	mọ́ládé	brings honour in
			864	mọ́làdé	brings wealth in
848	mó.sù	chooses Ifá divination power	865	mọ́ládùn	makes honour sweet
849	mósùn	acquires camwood	866	mọ́láyan	makes honour walk with pride
			867	mọ̀mí	knows me
850	mó.sùró	sustains divination	868	mọ́nà	mixes with craftsmanship
851	motẹ́rù	mine is a thing of awe or fright	869	mọ̀-ọ́nlọ̀	knows how to call people to worship
852	mówú	stops jealousy/envy	870	mọ̀-ọ́n-rìn	walks in at the right time
853	móyè	mixes with the throne (or chieftaincy)	871	mọ́rẹbísií	makes gifts to increase
			872	mọ̀rinlẹ̀	is popular
854	móyègún	sustains or straightens up the throne or chieftaincy	873	mọ́sẹ̀	takes the day of worship (Sabbath)
855	móyèlá	licks/swallows chieftaincy	874	mọ̀tẹ́rù	is enough as a thing of awe or fright
856	móyèró	sustains the throne or chieftaincy	875	mọ̀yìn	knows and appreciates praise
857	moyìn	I praise this deity			

	Predicate	Meaning		Predicate	Meaning
876	múbọni	holds firm in hand	896	múyìíwò	takes this for inspection or for a trial
877	múìíbí	takes this to give birth to	897	múyìwá	brings prestige in here
878	múlẹ̀	occupies the land	898	ḿwọnyì	measures and gives out prestige
879	újìmí	gives me totally			
880	múléró	sustains the house	899	náàíró	I am indebted to the divinity (Ìjẹ̀bú)
881	múlẹ̀gún	occupies the land to settle in permanently	900	náání	has respect for (me)
882	múná	is sharp			did not waste money, did not spend money (in vain)
883	múre	chooses what is good	901	.náwó (nu)
884	múrèlé	takes back home	902	náìkè	has wealth or prestige
885	múrewá	brings good luck	903	náiwo	is famous
886	músiré	takes to play with	904	námẹ̀	has a mark/ milestone
887	mútìmí	places with me to nurture	905	náriwo	is famous
888	mútuàbọ̀	brings back home	906	náyà	has courage
889	múwàgún	straightens posterity	907	náyé	possesses life/ the world
890	múyẹwò	takes on for inspection, or trial	908	náyéjù	possesses life most
			909	ñdé	mine has arrived
891	múyẹwọ́	uses (it) to dignify my hand	910	ñdélé	mine reaches home
892	múyì	takes on prestige	911	nẹ́kàn	has one (son)
893	muyìíbí	takes this on to give birth to	912	nẹ̀ẹ́gàn	does not have reproach
894	muyìíbọ̀	brings this back	913	nẹ́yẹ	has dignity
895	múyìíwá	brings this here	914	nẹ́yìn	has back bone, is strong

47

	Predicate	Meaning		Predicate	Meaning
915	níbùyan	has a place to walk with pride	935	nítorí	has a reason
916	níbọsun	is capable of increasing	936	nìwẹ̀	is a cleaner/ bather
917	nígà	has a palace	937	níyan	has pride
918	nìígàn	does not have reproach	938	níyè	has a thoughtful mind
919	nígba	has (200) very many children to give devotes	939	níyẹ	has to be dignified
			940	níyì	has prestige
920	nìígbàgbé	never forgets	941	níyọnu	causes a lot of trouble
921	níiwún	permits me to bluff	942	ñládé	mine has the crown
922	níji	has shade, is protective	943	ññíbẹ̀	is there always potent
923	níjọ	has a crowd	944	ñlẹ́gẹ́	is delicate
924	nìíkà	has no cruelty	945	ññítẹ̀ẹ́	mine has a throne
925	nikẹ̀ẹ́	has pampering			
926	nímokùn	adorns me with the coral bead wrist band	946	nóìkí	is famous
			947	.nọ̀ọ́jọ́	always potent, has no special day
927	nímọ̀	is wise, has knowledge			
928	níngbàyí-ṣemóore	says I should take this as a gift of kindness	948	.nòwó	did not spend money in vain, did not lose money
929	nìípẹkun	has no end	949	nọ́lá	has honour
930	níran	has ancestry	950	nọ́pé	deserves thanks
931	níranyè	has chieftaincy running in the family line	951	nọ̀rẹ̀n	does not lengthen my walk/ hardship
932	nìírègún	does not harp on favours done	952	.nọ̀rìn	same with nọ̀ rẹ̀n
933	nísí	has surplus (children)	953	nọ̀ọ́tẹ̀	is not rebellious
			954	nọ́wọ̀	has respect
934	nítẹ̀ẹ́	has a throne			

	Predicate	Meaning
955	ṅpé	mine is complete
956	ńpéjọ	is assembling
957	ńrelé	will reach home, or going home
958	ńrewájú	is progressing
959	ńṣẹ̀bẹ̀	is pleading my cause
960	.nù	is not lost, is still active
961	núbẹ̀	should be begged
962	núbi	has to be asked, should be asked
963	núbòsí	worthy of being cried to for help, has protection
964	núgà	has a palace
965	núgbà	worthy of being possessed
966	núkàsí	has to be recognized (Ìjẹ̀bú)
967	núlí	has a house (Òǹdó)
968	núpè	has to be called
969	núpèbi	has to be called and asked
970	núsì	has fame
971	núsi	has wealth, savings
972	òde	of the open, outside the entire populace
973	oge	the pretty

	Predicate	Meaning
974	òjó	male child with umbilical cord around his neck
975	òkun	ocean
976	omi	water
977	oróyè	on top of the throne
978	òsì	has not ceased (in the family)
979	òṣebikan	does not belong to only one place
980	òṣèké	does not deceive
981	òtí	does not fade, does not weaken
982	oyè	of the throne, of chieftaincy
983	ọlá	of honour
984	òṣun	of the river Ọ̀ṣun
985	pàdé	meet or mix
986	pamọ́	keeps this safe, protects this
987	pamílẹ́rìn-ín	makes me laugh
988	paríọlá	is the utmost of honour
989	pàṣẹ	commanded
990	.payè	does not kill memory
991	pé	is complete
992	pèé	is not complete
993	pègba	becomes two hundred (many)

	Predicate	Meaning		Predicate	Meaning
994	pegedé	excels superlatively	1014	pónmilé	flatters me
995	péjoyè	assembles to have chieftaincy title	1015	.pọ̀nà	does not destroy the road
996	péjú	is all present	1016	pọ̀tátán	destroys the enemy completely
997	pèlé	increases			
998	pétán	completely assembled	1017	.pọ̀tákù	does not leave any enemy alive
999	pẹ̀ẹ́	did not stay long behind before arriving	1018	pọ̀tun	creates a new one, becomes new
1000	pẹ̀	is not diminished	1019	putú	performs wonders
1001	(i)pẹ̀	consolatory	1020	rádéwò	finds a crown to look at
1002	pénúọlá	has been long in honour	1021	rádéwọ̀	finds a crown to wear
1003	pẹ́núṣọlá	delays birth to enjoy (in the womb)	1022	ralédoyè	buys a house for the throne or chieftaincy
1004	pẹ̀rọ̀	eases the situation	1023	rákinṣẹ́	sends the brave on an errand
1005	pẹtù	makes things easy	1024	rántí	remembers
1006	pẹtùn	makes things easy	1025	rántiolú	remembers olú
1007	pìtàn	narrates history, makes history	1026	ráyéwá	flourishes
			1027	refá	goes to or mixes with Ifá
1008	piti	vary many, voluminous	1028	relé	goes home
1009	pòlù	mixes	1029	rèlé	goes home (Oǹdó)
1010	pọ̀joyè	is more than chieftaincy	1030	rẹ̀mí	consoles me
1011	.pọ̀jù	not superfluous	1031	rẹ̀tán	pampers completely
1012	.pọlá	does not destroy honour	1032	ríbidó	finds a place to settle
1013	pọnñlé	flatters me			

	Predicate	Meaning
1033	ríbigbé	finds a place to live
1034	ríbọ́la	has enough to give to posterity
1035	rími	sees or finds me
1036	rímisi	sees or finds me more and more (with additional male birth)
1037	rímisìn	finds me as a worshipper
1038	rímọ̀	finds knowledge
1039	rìn	walks
1040	rìnádé	walks into the crown
1041	rìndé	walks in
1042	rìn-ín-re	walks well
1043	rìnládé	walks to possess the crown
1044	rinléwá	walks home
1045	rinléwò	does a trial walk of the house
1046	rìnlọ	does not walk away
1047	rìnlọ́lá	walks in honour
1048	rìnmádé	walks close to the crown
1049	rìnmọ́lá	walks close to honour
1050	rìnọlá	walks into honour
1051	rìn̄oyè	walks into chieftaincy

	Predicate	Meaning
1052	rìntọ́	walks right
1053	rínú	sees/knows (my) mind
1054	rìnwá	walks in here
1055	ríṣe	finds work to do
1056	ríyàn	finds to take/choose from
1057	ríyè	finds salvation
1058	ró	stays, waits
1059	ródoyè	waits for chieftaincy
1060	rógundé	sees war and arrives
1061	rójú	takes time; is not in a hurry
1062	.rojú	does not complain
1063	ròkànmí	thinks of me also
1064	rólíẹ	provides support for the house (Oǹdó)
1065	rómádé	waits to take the crown
1066	róunbí	finds something (good) to give birth to
1067	róminíyì	wraps me with prestige
1068	ròómojú	does not see tears
1069	.romójú	does not cause me pain
1070	róñkẹ	has something to pamper
1071	rore	thinks good/positive

	Predicate	Meaning
1072	rótanná	waits to light a lamp
1073	rótìbí	stays with pedigree
1074	rótìlú	stays/supports the town
1075	rótìmí	stays with me
1076	rótìmílọ́lá	stays with me in honour
1077	rótọ́lá	stays with honour
1078	róñbí	finds something good to give birth to
1079	róñgbé	finds something good to acquire
1080	róñkó	finds something good to collect
1081	róñmú	find something good to take (away)
1082	rògbà	supports with encirclement
1083	róyè	finds chieftaincy title
1084	rọ̀mádé	cleaves to the crown
1085	rọ́mọkẹ́	has a child to pamper
1086	rọ́pò	provides replacement
1087	rọ́rọ̀	find wealth
1088	rọ̀sótù	leans into otù, the supreme chieftaincy
1089	.rùkú	does not starve to death, has worshippers
1090	rùúkú	does not see death, survived

	Predicate	Meaning
1091	rúnkànmí	turns over to reach me
1092	rún-un-mú	finds something to take
1093	.runtán	is not exterminated
1094	sá	runs away
1095	sàá	does not run away
1096	sàga	creates a chair (personal abode)
1097	sálù	runs to, for protection, takes refuge
1098	sàmẹ̀	makes a mark
1099	sàmì	makes a mark
1100	sàn	is good, healthy
1101	san	pays, benefits
1102	sanjọ́	compensates/pays back for worshipping done
1103	sànlú	benefits the town
1104	sànmí	benefits me
1105	sànótù	benefits by making this birth easy
1106	sànóyè	is good for a chieftaincy
1107	sanwó	pays money back (used in making sacrifices)
1108	sànyà	compensates for ill-treatment

52

	Predicate	Meaning
1109	sanyè	benefits chieftaincy
1110	sèéùn	fulfilled its promise
1111	sìmbọ̀	follows me back
1112	simisọ́lá	rests inside honour
1113	.sìnrègún	does not harp on benefits given
1114	sogunró	suspends hostilities
1115	solú	follows olú (back)
1116	solúbọ̀	follows olú back
1117	sọjí	wakes up
1118	sọlédayọ̀	turns the home into joy
1119	sọmí	strikes me, aims at me to show its benevolence
1120	sọpé	says everything completely, has said it all
1121	sọrọ̀	makes wealth (Ìjẹ̀ṣà)
1122	.sọ̀yínù	shall not lose this (child)
1123	.súmbí	I am not tired of giving birth to
1124	súnkànmí	moves to reach me
1125	sùnlóyè	sleeps on top by chieftaincy
1126	sùnlọ́lá	sleeps on top of honour, has a lot of honour
1127	sùrójú	sleeps peacefully
1128	ṣáánú	shows mercy
1129	ṣadé	creates the crown
1130	.ṣaigbọ́	hears, does not pretend not to hear
1131	ṣakin	fights bravely
1132	ṣàndé	flows in
1133	ṣàní	chooses its possession
1134	.ṣànlọ	does not flow away
1135	ṣawẹ́	creates a "chip off the old block"
1136	ṣawẹ̀	makes the cleanser of barrenness
1137	ṣayọ̀	creates joy
1138	ṣeé	does it, I am grateful
1139	ṣeéhàn	is worthy of being exhibited
1140	ṣeémọ̀	is worthy of being known
1141	ṣéeni	is worthy of being possessed
1142	ṣeere	does well
1143	ṣeésìn	is worthy of being worshipped
1144	ṣegba	creates (200) many
1145	ṣèitán	completes this good deed, is wonderful

	Predicate	Meaning		Predicate	Meaning
1146	.ṣèké	is not fraudulent, did not deceive	1164	ṣèsan	compensates; provides a replacement
1147	ṣekọ́lá	adds to honour	1165	ṣèsọ̀	produces easy birth
1148	ṣèlú	manages the town properly	1166	.ṣètàn	did not deceive
1149	ṣemóore	is kind to me	1167	ṣétẹ̀	quells the rebellion
1150	ṣeun	does something good	1168	ṣẹtù	appeases
1151	.ṣemọ	did not stop blessing me	1169	ṣèyẹ	does the right thing, provides dignity
1152	ṣewéré	performs quickly	1170	ṣí	opens, starts
1153	ṣèyí	makes this happen, does this	1171	ṣidà	procures all-conquering sword
1154	ṣèyítán	makes this happen superlatively	1172	ṣígun	puts the army on the march, commences a war
1155	ṣèyójù	has done the most important/ appreciated	1173	ṣígbìn	opens the ìgbìn drum
1156	ṣègbọ́n	is superior (to other divinities)	1174	ṣiji	provides cover, protects
1157	ṣégun	conquers, wins the war	1175	ṣíjúadé	opens the face of the crown, initiates publicity of the crown, with this first birth
1158	ṣégunọ̀tá	conquers the enemy
1159	ṣèìndé	looks after his welfare in his absence	1176	ṣíjúwadé	opens its eyes to see the crown
1160	ṣèìndèmí	looks after my welfare in my absence	1177	ṣíjúwọla	opens its eyes to see honour
1161	ṣẹ̀mádé	originates with the crown	1178	ṣíkà	fulfills its promise
1162	ṣẹ̀mọ́wọ́	gives me the first one	1179	.ṣìkà	does not perform cruelty, is not cruel
1163	ṣẹ̀mọ́yìn	originates with praise

	Predicate	Meaning
1180	ṣíkù	has more left, remains, is not all finished
1181	ṣílé	opens the house, gives the first endowment to the family
1182	.ṣiléwọ̀	does not enter the wrong (unproductive) house
1183	ṣínà	opens the way/road
1184	ṣìpé	is not complete yet
1185	ṣìpẹ̀	consoles (with this child)
1186	ṣìyákàn	comes calling; visits us (Èkìtì)
1187	ṣiyan	moves and walks proudly
1188	ṣiyanbádé	moves and walks proudly to meet/join the crown
1189	ṣíyanbọ́là	moves and walks to meet honour
1190	ṣògo	creates glory
1191	ṣogun	creates/become an army
1192	ṣokùn	becomes/makes the wrist band of honour
1193	ṣoore	does kindness
1194	ṣòtítọ́	does the truth and fulfills promises

	Predicate	Meaning
1195	ṣowóolú	becomes the money (wealth) of Olú
1196	ṣògá	is supreme, becomes the master
1197	ṣògáolú	is superior to Olú
1198	ṣògbọ́n	makes wisdom
1199	.ṣògbọ́n	does not despise wisdom
1200	ṣọlá	creates honour, or enjoys honour actively
1201	ṣọlágbadé	receives the crown in the process of enjoying honour
1202	ṣọlápé	behaves honourably maximally
1203	ṣọ́lé	protects the house
1204	ṣọ́mojú	protects me
1205	ṣọmọ	creates a child
1206	ṣọmọgbì	creates a bouncing child easily
1207	ṣọ̀nà	creates the way
1208	ṣọrọ̀	creates wealth
1209	.ṣọ̀tẹ̀	is loyal, does not revolt
1210	ṣọwọ́bọ̀	brings back the hand, repairs
1211	.ṣọ̀wọ́n	does not create scarcity; not scarce

	Predicate	Meaning		Predicate	Meaning
1212	ṣọ́yè	watches over chieftaincy	1229	tàràwá	comes from Àrà, a town in Èkìtì
1213	ṣọ̀yìn	creates praises (for the family)	1230	tawúrà	sells gold, displays gold (with this child's birth)
1214	ṣùbòmí	crowds me pleasantly			
1215	ṣùpọ̀	assembles			
1216	sùsì	creates fame	1231	táyọ̀	is worthy of being joyful about
1217	ṣùtán	assembles completely	1232	téṣù	is as powerful as Èṣù
1218	ṣùwà	creates posterity	1233	tẹ̀ẹ́	does not lose respect
1219	táańwá	that we have been looking for	1234	.tẹ̀	stays upright, does not lose dignity
1220	tádé	is as valuable as the crown; is up to a crown	1235	tẹ̀	changes its mind; yields to pressure to give us this child
1221	tádéṣe	uplifts the crown, repairs the crown			
1222	tàjòbọ̀	comes back from a journey	1236	tẹ́gbẹ́	is any comrade's equal
1223	tàjòlà	becomes wealthy during a journey, or away from home	1237	tẹ́jú	is plain with no guise
			1238	tẹ́júoṣó	publicizes the wise seer
1224	tamílọrẹ	gives me a gift	1239	tẹ̀là	settles down and becomes rich
1225	.tamínù	does not reject me	1240	tẹ̀lú	arrives the town, founds a town
1226	tàn-án	is not finished; remains			
1227	tányérọ	reshapes the life of the family	1241	tẹluwò	enters the town to see (if it is good)
1228	tàràdé	comes from Àrà, a town in Èkìtì	1242	tẹ̀mẹ́kún	stops my weeping
			1243	.tẹ́mi	does not disappoint me

	Predicate	Meaning
1244	tèmọ́wọ́	reaches my hand
1245	téníọlá	spreads out a sleeping mat of honour
1246	tèrìnwá	comes from "Èrìn" a town in Ìjẹ̀sà land
1247	tẹ́rù	is worth being feared
1248	tèsọ́lá	bends into honour
1249	.tẹ́ṣu	did not ridicule Èṣù
1250	tẹ́tí	listens
1251	tiba	settles with father
1252	tibọ̀	has come back
1253	tidébẹ̀	has reached the place
1254	.tìgbé	has not perished, is still active
1255	tíílọ	has not all gone from the family, remains
1256	tìlọ	same as tíílọ
1257	tiléwá	has come from home (town)
1258	tìmiléyìn	supports me
1259	timírìn	has grown up, is walking
1260	.tìmójú	does not make me to be ashamed; supports
1261	tinúoyè (wá)	comes from inside chieftaincy
1262	tińwọ́	has become many
1263	.tìrègún	does not harp on favours granted
1264	titómiládé	is enough for me as a crown
1265	tóbi	is big/ large/ powerful
1266	tófúnmi	is enough for me
1267	togunbọ̀	comes from war (first child by wife captured in war)
1268	tókè	is as powerful, or as constant as the mountain
1269	tóókọ̀yà	powerful enough to recompense ill-treatment
1270	tókun	is up to the ocean, is as expansive as the ocean
1271	tókùn	is as honourable as the coral-bead wrist-cord
1272	tòkunbọ̀	comes back from the ocean
1273	tolú	stays with Olú
1274	tólú	is as worthy as Olú
1275	tómi	is enough for me

	Predicate	Meaning		Predicate	Meaning
1276	tómiísìn	is enough as my deity to worship	1291	tòrò	is crystal clear
1277	tómiláde	is enough for me as my crown	1292	tóówún	is enough to bluff with
			1293	tóyì	is enough for prestige
1278	tómilólá	is enough for mea as honour	1294	tóyè	as prestigious as chieftaincy title
1279	tóògùn	is as powerful and effective as medicine	1295	tóyèbí	has reborn chieftaincy title
1280	tóókí	is worthy of being greeted in worship	1296	tóyìnbó	is as precious and good as a European
1281	tòóròbí	gives birth in the morning	1297	tóba	is up to a king in value; is as worthy as a king
1282	tóósìn	is enough as an item of worship			
1283	tóówò	is worthy of looking up to	1298	todúnwá	comes from the annual festival
1284	tóówojú	is worthy of looking up to; being used as a saviour	1299	tójúolá	takes care of honour
			1300	tólá	is enough as honour
1285	tóówún	is worthy of bluffing with	1301	tolámí	breathes from honour
1286	tóóyàn	is worthy of being selected as an item of worship	1302	tòmí	comes to me
			1303	tòmídé	comes to me, and arrives
1287	tóóyìn	is worthy of being praised	1304	tòmíwá	comes to me, and arrives
1288	tóóyòmó	is worthy of cleaving to in joy	1305	tònàdé	comes in from the road/journey
1289	tóóyòsí	is worthy of being joyous towards	1306	tósóyè	is fit for a chieftaincy
			1307	tòtè	subdues conspiracy
1290	tóríolá	is worthy of being the head of honour	1308	towóbolá	dips hand in honour

	Predicate	Meaning
1309	tọyóbọ̀	comes back from Ọ̀yọ́ (the town)
1310	túbọ̀	comes back again
1311	túbọ̀sún	increases further
1312	túfaratì	is enough to lean on as support
1313	túgbìíyèlé	is enough to depend on
1314	túgbẹ̀ẹ́yèlé	dialect variant of túgbìíyèlé
1315	tugbóbọ̀	comes back from the bush
1316	túgbọ	expels gloom/sadness
1317	túkàsí	is enough to reckon with
1318	túkìí	is enough to greet in worship
1319	tulà	escapes to survive and become wealthy
1320	túlà	is enough to become wealthy with
1321	tùmínínú	comforts me
1322	tùmínú	comforts me
1323	tún-àṣe	makes posterity better
1324	túnbọ̀	comes back again
1325	túndé	comes back
1326	túndùn	is sweet gain
1327	túngàṣe	makes the palace look good, repairs the palace
1328	túnjí	wakes up again
1329	túnríyèlé	finds again to make the home healthy (with no leaking roof)
1330	túnwàṣe	makes behavior better
1331	túríyèlé	finds again to make the home healthy
1332	túnríyẹlé	finds again to dignify the house with
1333	túròótì	is enough to stay/settle with
1334	túsààlù	is powerful enough to run to for protection
1335	túsì	is enough for fame
1336	tútì	is enough to lean on for support
1337	tutù	is peaceful, is not aggressive
1338	túwò	is enough to look up to
1339	túyàn	is enough to be chosen for worship
1340	túyẹn	is worthy of being praised
1341	túyì	is enough for prestige
1342	túyọ̀	is enough to be joyful about

	Predicate	Meaning
1343	túyọmọ́	is enough to flutter towards in joy
1344	wájánàọlá	comes to make the road to honour clear
1345	wájánàọlà	comes to make the road to wealth clear
1346	wájayéọlá	comes to enjoy a life of honour
1347	wálé	comes home
1348	wáñdé	searches for me to find me here
1349	wáñwá	searches for me; visits me
1350	wáwawá	comes searching for us; visits us
1351	wáre	fetches good luck
1352	wáyé	comes to life
1353	wáyìí(dé)	searches for this
1354	wépọ̀	combines together
1355	wẹ̀dé	swims to arrive here
1356	wẹmímọ́	exonerates me, washes me clean
1357	wẹnù	washes up (the stigma of childlessness)
1358	wẹnùmọ́	washes up clean (stigma of childlessness)
1359	wẹ̀yà	cleans up ill-treatment or undeserved punishment

	Predicate	Meaning
1360	wẹ̀yinmi	cleans up my after-here, gives me a successor
1361	wíbẹ́ẹ̀	said so
1362	wìnmí	pleases me (to own)
1363	wòó	takes care
1364	.wolétì	is capable of guarding the house
1365	wolú	enters the Olú family
1366	wòlú	guards the town
1367	wòmílójú	pities me
1368	woore	takes cognizance of (my) kindness
1369	wore	looks at something good
1370	wòtù	enters the Otù chieftaincy
1371	wọ̀	enters, or is appropriate
1372	wọbí	is easy to give birth to
1373	wọbí	enters the family/pedigree
1374	wọbi	is proper to be asked (for a child)
1375	wọ̀gà	enters the palace
1376	wọlé	enters the house
1377	wọ́kímiwá	comes in a crowd to greet me

	Predicate	Meaning		Predicate	Meaning
1378	wọlú	enters the town (large family)	1396	yalé	comes to the house
1379	wọ́nmi	is scarce for me. I am short of	1397	yàlé	comes to the house (Ìjẹ̀bú)
1380	.wọ́nmi	I have enough of; I am not short of	1398	yalémi	comes to my house
			1399	.yalọ	does not split away
1381	wọyè	enters chieftaincy	1400	yanjú	is clear (of conflict)
1382	wọ̀yìn	enters into praise	1401	yànmíwò	chooses me to visit
1383	wùmí	is liked by me	1402	yànńwò	chooses me to visit
1384	wùmíísìn	pleases me to worship	1403	yè	prospers; survives
1385	wùnmí	is liked by me			
1386	wùmiílò	I enjoy using the named divinity	1404	yèbí	sustains the family line or pedigree
			1405	yèbọ́	is free from encumbrances
1387	.wunmí	gives me no negative consequence; repercussion	1406	yètán	prospers/ survives completely
1388	wùsì	is loved by publicity/ fame	1407	yẹ	befits
1389	wùsi	is loved by wealth/ savings	1408	yẹ̀ba	befits the family sanctuary
1390	wúwo	is heavy/ prestigious	1409	yẹbí	befits the family line
1391	wuyè	is loved by chieftaincy	1410	yẹfá	befits Ifá
			1411	yẹgbẹ́	befits comrades
1392	wuyì	is loved by prestige	1412	yẹ̀gẹ̀	is fit to be pampered
1393	yàgò	turns out to be a protector (chicken coop)	1413	.yẹ̀gẹ̀	does not change/stop its pampering
1394	yakin	turns out to be a warrior	1414	yẹkún	stops weeping
1395	.yànkin (nù)	does not desert the brave	1415	yẹlé	befits the house

	Predicate	Meaning		Predicate	Meaning
1416	yèlú	benefits/befits the town	1434	yínká	is all around me
1417	yẹlú	befits the King, Olú	1435	yìntó	has praised us superbly
1418	yèlúrẹ̀	benefits his/her town; befits its town	1436	yíólú	mixes with Olú
			1437	yíóyè	rolls or turns into chieftaincy
1419	yẹmí	befits me			
1420	yẹmíjù	befits me superlatively	1438	yípò	changes unfortunate position (of childlessness)
1421	yẹ̀míwò	examines me, or visits me	1439	yíwọlá	rolls into honour
1422	yẹmọ	befits a child	1440	yọ̀ádé	rejoices at being joined with the crown
1423	yẹ́misí	honours me; pays me respect			
			1441	yọdé	emerges
1424	yẹni	befits a person	1442	yọkùn	celebrates the wrist-band chieftaincy
1425	yẹ̀nwò	examines me or visits me			
1426	yẹra	befits the body	1443	yọ̀lé	makes the home joyous
1427	yẹrí	befits the head	1444	yòmádé	rejoices at seeing the crown
1428	yẹsí	respects it (child)			
1429	yẹwọ́	befits to hold in hand	1445	yọḿbọ̀	brings me back safely
1430	yígà	is all over the palace	1446	yọmí	saves me
			1447	yọ̀ọ́lá	rejoices at honour
1431	yììgà`	does not change the palace	1448	yọrúwà	excels in good behavior
1432	yíkànmí	rolls to reach me to be my turn	1449	yòsótù	rejoices at otù chieftaincy
1433	yímbíti	surrounds me plentifully	1450	yọye	celebrates chieftaincy

Non-Divinity and Non-Totem Nouns as Subjects of Yorùbá sentence-names (with common predicates)

	Subject	Meaning
1)	Àgbè	farm district that is very fertile and makes people live prosperous lives. It used to be of such significance in the lives of the inhabitants that they named children with it. For example: Ọpẹ́agbè (thanks to Àgbè), or use it as the subject of sentence names.

	Common Predicates	Meaning
1	bí	gives birth (to this child)
2	bíyìi	gives birth to this
3	gbọlá	receives honour
4	láyọ̀	has joy
5	lúsi	has wealth
6	sìnmíbọ̀	follows me back home
7	şakin	creates the brave
8	tọ́lá	is as good as honour
9	yẹmí	befits me, makes me prosperous
10	yìnmí	praises me
11	lúyì	has prestige
12	sanmí	is beneficial/enriching to me
13	sànwá	is beneficial/enriching to us
14	sanwá	dialect variation of sànwá

	Subject	Meaning
2)	Àgbẹ̀	Farming
	Common Predicates	**Meaning**
1	lúyì	has prestige
2	sanmí	is beneficial/enriching to me
3	sànwá	is beneficial/enriching to us
4	sanwá	dialect variation of sànwá

	Subject	Meaning
3)	Àjé	Money/Investment
	Common Predicates	**Meaning**
1	báñdélé	gets home with me
2	dé	has arrived
3	gbèé	is not lost
4	iígbé	never gets lost
5	níya	has insults
6	pé	is profitable
7	túnmọbí	reshapes a child's character, remoulds a person
8	wọlé	enters the house
9	wùmí	pleases me
10	yalémi	branches into my house

4)

Subject	Meaning
Ayé	Life (the world)

	Common Predicates	Meaning
1	dùn	is sweet
2	gbẹgẹ́	is delicate
3	gbùsì	accepts fame
4	ọ̀la	of posterity (tomorrow)
5	pọlá	destroys/kills honour
6	yí	changes (for the better)

5)

Subject	Meaning
Ayọ̀	Joy

	Common Predicates	Meaning
1	bámi	meets/joins me
2	dèji	becomes two
3	délé	reaches home (with me)
4	kúnlé	fills the house
5	kúnmi	fills me
6	kúnnú	fills inside me
7	ọlá	of honour
8	pọ̀síi	increases
9	rindé	walked to arrive
10	túndé	comes again
11	yínká	surrounds me

	Subject	Meaning
6)	Baba	Father or God
	Common Predicates	**Meaning**
1	bùnmi	gives me (as a gift)
2	dé	arrives
3	déyìnbọ̀	comes back
4	fẹ́mi	loves me
5	fúnmi	gives me to give birth to
6	fúnñbí	gives me to give birth to
7	fúnñkẹ́	gives me to pamper
8	fúnñtọ́	gives me to bring up
9	ríñsá	sees me and runs away (dies)
10	rínú	knows my mind, my wishes
11	ṣ ọlá	creates honour
12	tàjòdé	comes back from a journey, comes back from a distant place
13	táyọ̀	is enough to be joyful about
14	túndé	comes again

	Subject	Meaning
7)	Èlú	The town
	Common Predicates	**Meaning**
1	bánji	wakes up with me in support
2	dire	turns out good
3	loyè	is chieftaincy
4	moyè	recognizes chieftaincy
5	mọ̀ọ́ká	knows it all around
6	yẹmí	befits me
7	yọ̀mádé	rejoices at the crown

	Subject	Meaning
8)	Ewé	Leaf/Herb/Medicine/Herbalism
	Common Predicates	**Meaning**
1	bíyìí	gives birth to this
2	dèmi	binds me, keeps me alive
3	dùnmóyè	is sweet in addition to chieftaincy
4	jẹ́	is efficacious
5	múná	is sharp, is efficacious
6	pẹtù	eases the situation

	Subject	Meaning
9)	Ẹ̀san	Vengeance
	Common Predicates	**Meaning**
1	gbẹ̀dọ̀	needs to be pursued thoughtfully/carefully
2	júùgbà	cannot be effected

10)	Subject		Meaning
	Ìfẹ́		Love
	Common Predicates		**Meaning**
	1	dàpọ̀	mixes up, combines
	2	làjà	ends the quarrel
	3	layọ̀	is joy
	4	láyọ̀	has joy
	5	lẹ́yẹ	has dignity
	6	lọ́wọ̀	has respect
	7	olúwa	of God
	8	túgà	is as good as a palace
	9	yìnwá	praises us

11)	Subject		Meaning
	Igbó		The forest/farmland
	Common Predicates		**Meaning**
	1	lọ́lá	has honour
	2	nírè	is profitable
	3	sanmi	benefits me
	4	sànyà	compensates suffering
	5	yẹmí	befits me

12)

	Subject	Meaning
	Ikú	Death

	Common Predicates	**Meaning**
1	dalénù	scatters the house
2	.dẹ̀yìnbọ̀	does not come back
3	éèsàn	is bad
4	.jẹ́ñyọ̀	does not allow me to rejoice
5	mẹniísàn	has taken a very good person
6	mẹniísan	does not differentiate between good and bad people
7	múyi	takes away prestige
8	nùúyì	has no prestige
9	òmẹniísàn	does not know the difference between a good person and a bad person, it kills every one alike
10	pẹléyẹ	kills the dignified
11	polúyì	kills the prestigious
12	runmí	does not exterminate me
13	şìkà	does something wicked
14	yànmójú	makes me anxious

13)

	Subject	Meaning
	Ìlú	The town
	Common Predicates	**Meaning**
1	dire	turns out good
2	loyè	is chieftaincy
3	moyè	recognises chieftaincy
4	mọ̀ọ́ká	knows it all around
5	yẹmí	befits me
6	yọ̀mádé	rejoices at the crown

14)

	Subject	Meaning
	Ìwà	Character
	Common Predicates	**Meaning**
1	lẹ̀sin	is religion
2	lẹwà	is beauty
3	loyè	is chieftaincy

15)

	Subject	Meaning
	Iyì	Prestige
	Common Predicates	**Meaning**
1	ladé	is the crown
2	ọlá	of honour

16)

	Subject	Meaning
	Ogun	War
	Common Predicates	**Meaning**
1	dalénù	scatters the home
2	fàyàn	causes famine
3	fólùú	destroys the town
4	mákindé	brings the brave
5	mákinlọ	takes away the brave
6	pọlátì	cannot destroy honour
7	.pọlátán	does not destroy honour completely

17)

	Subject	Meaning
	Ojú	The eye
	Common Predicates	**Meaning**
1	kòtì	is not ashamed
2	kùúròlọ́lá	has not stopped looking at honour
3	ọlá	of honour
4	ọlápé	of honour assembles completely
5	.ríbi	does not see evil
6	romí	pains me (at the absence of a beloved one)
7	tikú	death is ashamed

	Subject	Meaning
18)	Olúwa / Olú	Lord God

	Common Predicates	Meaning
1	bùkánlá bùkọ́lá	adds to honour
2	bùsọ́lá	adds to honour
3	dámiláre	justifies me
4	fẹ́mi	loves me
5	fúnmi	gives me
6	kẹ́mi	pampers me
7	máyọ̀wá	brings joy
8	múyẹmí	takes (this) to give me dignity
9	ṣèyí	does this
10	ṣínà	opens the way
11	tùmínínú	consoles me
12	rótìmí	stays with me
13	ṣẹ́gunọ̀tá	conquers the enemy
14	túyì	is enough as prestige

19)

	Subject	Meaning
	Owó	Money
	Common Predicates	**Meaning**
1	bọ́rọ̀dé	arrives with wealth
2	dùn- ún-ní	is sweet to have
3	ẹ̀yẹ	of dignity
4	labí	is what we gave birth to
5	lòwò	is business / commerce
6	lọlá	is honour
7	ṣílé	finishes the building/opens the house
8	.tọmọ	is not as valuable as a child
9	tùmí	makes things easy for me
10	yẹlé	befits the house

20)

	Subject	Meaning
	Oyin	Honey
	Common Predicates	**Meaning**
1	dàmọ́lá	mixes with honour
2	dépò	reaches its goal
3	jọ́láyẹmí	lets honour befit me
4	kánsọ́lá	drops into honour
5	kúnlé	fills the house
6	ladùn	the joy is as sweet as honey
7	loyè	chieftaincy is as sweet as honey
8	lọlá	honour is as sweet as honey

21)	Subject		Meaning
	Ọlá		Honour
	Common Predicates		**Meaning**
1	bámijí		wakes up with me
2	báñjí		wakes up with me
3	bíyìí		gave birth to this
4	dépò		reaches the right position
5	dòkun		becomes vast (the ocean)
6	ẹ̀gbọ́n		honour of a senior brother or sister
7	Ifá		of the divination deity
8	ìyá		of the mother
9	kúnlé		fills the house
10	lọmí		is great
11	níyì		has prestige
12	ọ̀fẹ́		free honour
13	ọ̀rẹ́		of a friend
14	ṣílé		opens the house
15	sìmbọ̀		follows me back (home)
16	túndé		comes again
17	wọyè		enters chieftaincy
18	wọyin		enters into honey
19	yíwọlá		rolls into other honour

	Subject	Meaning
22)	Ọlọ́run	God
	Common Predicates	**Meaning**
1	fẹ́mi	loves me
2	fúnmi	gives me
3	lógbọ́n	is the only wise one
4	níìṣọlá	is the only one who creates honour
5	tóóyìn	is enough to be praised
6	yọmí	saves me

	Subject	Meaning
23)	Ọmọ	Child
	Common Predicates	**Meaning**
1	boríowó	is superior to money
2	boríọlá	is superior to honour
3	bọ̀ádé	comes back into the crown
4	bọ́lájí	wakes up with honour
5	bọ́láńlé	meets honour at home
6	bọ́lápé	assembles with (other honour), or "bọ́lá" is complete
7	bọ́láòtán	"bọ́lá" is not finished yet
8	búléjọ	befits the house
9	dán	glitters / shines beautifully
10	dára	is good
11	dùn- ún-bí	is sweet to give birth to
12	dùn- ún-kẹ́	is sweet to pamper
13	dùn- ún -ní	is sweet to have

	Subject	Meaning
23)	Ọmọ	Child
	Common Predicates	**Meaning**
14	dùn- ún-wò	is sweet to take care of
15	jáde	come out
16	jọlá	enjoys honour
17	jọlà	enjoys wealth
18	juadé	is more valuable than crown
19	jùwà	more valuable than (good) character
20	kówàjọ	assembles posterity (family)
21	là	survives
22	làbákẹ́	is the thing to pamper
23	ladé	is the crown
24	ladùn	is sweetness
25	lará	is relations / relatives
26	laríwò	is the one we see to take care of
27	.láyọ̀lé	is not worthy of being joyful over
28	le	is hard (to find)
29	lẹ̀yìnwá	is the future
30	lòfin	is the one that is compulsory to have
31	lokùn	is coral writs-band chieftaincy
32	lójù	is the most important
33	loyè	is chieftaincy
34	nìgbẹ̀yìn	is the one that survives one
35	nipò	is social status

	Subject		Meaning
23)	Ọmọ		Child
	Common Predicates		**Meaning**
	36	niyì	is prestige
	37	nìwà	is good character
	38	nùúyọ̀lé	is not worth being joyous over
	39	paríọlá	is the end all of honour
	40	róláwún	sees honour and bluffs
	41	sinmí	buries / survives me
	42	ṣọ̀wọ́n-ẹni	are scarce for us
	43	.ṣọ̀wọ́n-ẹni	are not scarce for us
	44	ṣulé	makes up the home
	45	ṣeébí	is possible to give birth to
	46	tárá	is equivalent to relatives
	47	táyọ̀	is equivalent to joy
	48	tánbàjẹ́	ends ridicules / shame
	49	téjì	is good enough to be a partner, or is as good as two people
	50	tọ́ṣọ̀ọ́	is enough as ornament
	51	tọ́ba	is as valuable as a king
	52	tóóbora	is enough to be one's cover-cloth / protection
	53	tóríọlá	can head all honour
	54	túbora	is enough as cover-cloth
	55	wá	comes
	56	wáyé	comes to the world

	Subject	Meaning
23)	Ọmọ	Child
Common Predicates		**Meaning**
57	worarẹ̀	takes care of itself
58	wọn	is precious, or scarce
59	wọnúọlá	enters into honour
60	wùmí	is liked by me
61	wùnmí	is liked by me
62	yájowó	is easier to have than money, or more precious than money
63	yẹni	befits us
64	yọlá	exhibits honour

	Subject	Meaning
24)	Ọ̀pá	Drumstick
Common Predicates		**Meaning**
1	bùnmi	gives me
2	kúnlé	fills the house
3	lékè	excels
4	níran	has pedigree
5	níyì	has dignity
6	ṣíji	casts a protective shadow
7	wùmí	is liked by me
8	yẹlé	befits the house
9	yẹmí	befits me
10	yìnmí	gives me praise

	Subject	Meaning
25)	Ọpẹ́	Thanks/Gratitude
	Common Predicates	**Meaning**
1	àgbè	(to Àgbè), uniquely fertile district in Àkókó or Ìjẹ̀ṣà areas
2	bọ̀dé	comes back
3	ìyá	of mother
4	mììpọ̀	is much
5	yẹfá	befits Ifá
6	yẹmí	is good for me to give

	Subject	Meaning
26)	Ọ̀rẹ́	Friendship
	Common Predicates	**Meaning**
1	dàpọ̀	mixes up, becomes one
2	dẹbí	becomes family
3	dẹgbẹ́	becomes comradeship
4	dèyìnbọ̀	comes back
5	.dẹ̀ìn	did not desert (me)
6	dọlá	becomes honour

	Subject	Meaning
27)	Òtẹ̀	War/rebellion – names used by descendants of Ìjẹ̀bù people born after the Òwìwí war
	Common Predicates	**Meaning**
1	dọlá	becomes honour
2	gbèmi	is beneficial to me
3	gbẹ́yẹ	takes away family dignity
4	gbẹ̀yẹ	becomes dignified
5	màákin	did not take the brave
6	mákin(lọ)	took the brave (away)
7	nìígbàgbé	cannot be forgotten
8	túlé	scatters the home
9	tùúlé	did not scatter the home

	Subject	Meaning
28)	Ọwá	The King
	Common Predicates	**Meaning**
1	dayọ̀	becomes joy
2	délé	gets home
3	dìmẹ́yìn	supports me
4	tàjòdé	comes back from a journey/distant town
5	tilèwá	comes from home

Àmútọ̀runwá (Names Brought From Heaven)

	Name	Meaning
1.	Aása	Child that cries incessantly, at night only
2.	Àbátàn	Child received from Òrìṣà Odò/ Òrìṣà Omi after worship
3.	Abíára	Child whose father dies before pregnancy was conspicuous on mother, and definitely born not later than nine months after father's death
4.	Abíba	Gives birth to the (dead) grandfather
5.	Abíìbá	Daughter born shortly after the father's death
6.	Abíodún	Born during an annual festival
7.	Abíọ̀nà	Born on the way, during a journey
8.	Abíọṣẹ	Born on the day of worship of God, or named deity
9.	Abọ́sẹ̀dé	She who arrives with the Sabbath day of God, or named deity
10.	Àdùbí	see Ìgè
11.	Àìná	Female child born with umbilical cord around her neck, is so named in all Yorùbá ethnic groups except the Ìjẹ̀bú who give the name to both sexes.
12.	Àjàsá	Child born covered with the caul of water-bag except for its head and feet
13.	Àjàyí	Child born face downwards
14.	Akálà	see Sàlákọ
15.	Àlàbá	Female child after Ìdòwú, traditionally second child born after a set of twins

	Name	Meaning
16.	Amósùn	Male child born from Ìrosùntúá pregnancy
17.	Amúsàn-án	Male child born with the head totally covered with eh water-bag membrane like a masquerade
18.	Ato	Female child born with the water-bag covering the head completely like a masquerade
19.	Àyọ̀ká	Child born from pregnancy after sacrifice to Ìwòrì- méjì at divination when searching for pregnancy
20.	Babádé	Father has come. First male child after father's or grandfather's death
21.	Babarímisá	Male child whose father dies during the first week of life
22.	Babárìndé	Father walks in. First male child born three or more years after the grandfather's death
23.	Babaríñsá	see Babarímisá
24.	Babátúndé	Father has come again. A reincarnation of a grandfather
25.	Babatúnjí	Father wakes up again, born shortly after father's death
26.	Babáyalé	Child born shortly after grandfather's death or grand uncle's death
27.	Babáyẹju	Father takes his eyes away, male child born very shortly after the father's death
28.	Dàda	Child with knotted hairs (the modern Rasta dreadlocks)
29.	Dọ̀pẹ̀mú	Female child born from an Òtúáròsùn pregnancy
30.	Eleeko	Female child from an Odù Ìrẹtẹ̀ròsùn pregnancy
31.	Ekìnnẹ̀	Child with very soft hairs like the cat's

	Name	Meaning
32.	Erinlẹ	Child whose umbilical cord is wrapped around a hand, a leg or waist as follows: Erinlẹ Ojútù- right hand Erinlẹ Abátan- left hand Erinlẹ Igberi- right leg ErinlẹOńdù- left leg Erinlẹ Oso – waist
33.	Ẹdun	One of twin children
34.	Ẹtaòkò	The third child in a set of triplets
35.	(I)Gínsanrín	Child with conspicuously spiral umbilical cord
36.	Gbáńgbálà	Child (male or female) from an Odù Ọ̀kànràntúá pregnancy
37.	Ìdògbé	Male child born after Ìdòwú but the name is now out of use
38.	Ìdòwú	The child after the twins male or female
39.	Ìfàni	Child born after Ìrúnní. Fifth child after Òní
40.	Ìgé (Àdùbí)	Child born with a leg-presentation during labour
41.	Ìjeni	Child born after Ìfàni. Sixth child after Òní
42.	Iwinlọlá	Female child born as a result of pregnancy from a divination that produced Ogbègúndá when searching for the pregnancy
43.	Odù	Child born with six toes on each foot (see Olúgbodi)
44.	Ojútù	See Erinlẹ
45.	Ìlọrí	Child whose pregnancy occurred at a time when the mother had not menstruated for very many years since the birth of the last

	Name	Meaning
		child
46.	Ìrèní	Child born after Ọtúnla. Third child after Òní
47.	Ìrúnní	Child born after Ìrèní. Fourth child after Òní
48.	Ìyábọ̀ (de)	Mother has come. First female child born after grandmother's death
49.	Ìyábọ̀wálé	Mother has come back home (same as Ìyábọ̀)
50.	Jọ̀họ́jọ̀	Male child whose mother died during labour or within a week after birth
51.	Jọ̀ọ́dá	Name given to a child recognized as àbíkú through Òdù Ọ̀yẹ̀kú Jọ̀ọ́dá at divination before birth
52.	Jọ̀ọ́jọ̀	See Jọ̀họ́jọ̀
53.	Kẹ́indé	The second (later) child in a set of twins
54.	Òhúù	Child born with six fingers on each hand (see Olúgbodi)
55.	Òjó	Male child born with the umbilical cord around his neck in all Yorùbá ethnic groups, except Ìjẹ̀bú who never give the name to their children
56.	Òkè	Child that always faints if being force-fed and thrives strictly only on cold water. No medicine, no warm water baths and no herbal hot water to drink, no forced feeding.
57.	Olúgbódi	Child born with six fingers on each hand and six toes on each foot
58.	Òní	Child that did not cry quickly or cried incessantly day and night, until the cognomen of Òní was recited on him

	Name	Meaning
59.	Oróyè	Child that cries incessantly at night only. The Ẹgba use the name mostly
60.	Ọdúnjọ	Child born after Ìrẹ́tẹ̀gúndá to an Awo father from divination on what the coming festival would be like
61.	Ọdúnm̀bákù	Name given to a child as prescribed by the diviner if the corpus Èjìogbè appears for the mother when in search of pregnancy
62.	Òkẹ́	Child born totally covered with the caul or water-bag membrane
63.	Òkẹ́owó	Bag of money. Child born totally covered with the caul or water-bag membrane. The owó (money) was originally a jocular appendage
64.	Ọla	Child born after Òní
65.	Òlọ́sun	See Òkè
66.	Ọmọ́pẹ́	Child born after an unusually long gestation
67.	Ọmọ́pẹ́nú	Child born after an unusually long gestation
68.	Ońdù	See Erinlẹ̀
69.	Oso	See Erinlẹ̀
70.	Òtúnla	Child born after Ọla. Second child after Òní
71.	Pẹ́-ń-nú	Child born after an unusually long gestation
72.	Sàlàkọ́	Child born with umbilical cord up over the shoulder to the back and around the waist (see Tàlàbí)
73.	Sàndà	Child born from a pregnancy that was had as a result of Ògúndá méjì and its sacrifice, when the diviner was consulted

	Name	Meaning
74.	Táí	First child in a set of twins
75.	Táíwò	First child in a set of twins
76.	Tàlàbí	Child born with the umbilical cord up over the shoulder to the back and around the waist (see Sàlàkọ́), or child for whom immaculate white cloth was hung before Òrìṣàńlà for his pregnancy to occur
77.	Táyé	First child in a set of twins
78.	Yésìdé	Female child born shortly after the death of any of the two grandmothers
79.	Yerímisá	Female child whose mother died on the day of birth
80.	Yetúndé	First female child born after the death of the grandmother by any of the children
81.	Yewañdé	Same as Yetúndé

Situationally Created Names (Bí-ígbàá-ti-rí orúkọ Adásọmọ)

	Name	Meaning and Circumstances
1.	Àánú	Mercy, (of Olú or Olúwa - God)
2.	Àanúolú	Mercy of Olú originally the paramount chief, but taken since the introduction of Christianity to mean the shortened form of Olúwa – Lord God.
3	Àárínadé	The middle of crowns (Adé); at least three older children whose names start with Adé had been born.
4.	Àárínolú	The middle of Olú, at least three older children whose names start with Olú had been born.
5.	Àárínoṣó	The middle of Oṣó, at least three older children whose names start with Oṣó had been born
6.	Àbádáhùnsí	We would have contributed to settling the quarrel (that probably had to do with the pregnancy or involved the child's parents)
7.	Àbátàn(mí)	I would have been deceived (over the pregnancy, or deceit almost happened, but did not)
8.	Àbáyọmí	I would have been ridiculed (over a family tragedy that almost happened, but did not)
9.	Abéégúndé	He that arrived with Eégún (masquerade) – a child born at the beginning or during the Eégún festival
10.	Abéégúnrìn	Same as Abéégúndé
11.	Abéjidé	He that arrived with the rain – a child born during a heavy downpour or on the day of the first rain in the year
12.	Abíálà	Born unto the deity whose insignia is immaculate white cloth

	Name	Meaning and Circumstances
13.	Abíára	We have given birth to an addition to our body (family)
14.	Àbídákun	Born to pacify (a quarrel in the family)
15.	Abídèmí	Child born when the father was away on a journey
16.	Abídogun	Male child born to wait the occurrence of a war, or born to fight, or born to become a militant
17.	Abídoyè	Born to await the chieftaincy title that is imminent
18.	Abífárìn	One who walked (in) with the Ifá oracle – child born at the beginning of the Ifá worship or festival
19.	Abímbólú	My birth connotes the birth of honour, or I was born to meet honour
20.	Abímbọ́lá	Same as Abímbólú
21.	Abíọ́dùn	Child born during an annual festival; any annual festival
22.	Abíórò	We have given birth to an addition to Orò, the totem of the "curfew cult" families
23.	Abíóyè	Born into chieftaincy or born as an addition to chieftaincy
24.	Abíọ́là	We have given birth to an addition to our honour
25.	Abíọ́nà	Born physically by the roadside
26.	Abíọ́rọ̀	Born into wealth
27.	Abíọ́sẹ̀	Born on a day of the worship of the family Deity or Christian God.
28.	Abírí	We have given birth before (name given to a child whose birth was accompanied with unusually difficult labour)
29.	Abísárá	We have given birth to an addition to our relatives

	Name	Meaning and Circumstances
30.	Abísógun	Born into a war or family quarrel, or born during a war or family quarrel
31.	Abísóyè	Born into a chieftaincy title, or we have born an addition to the Oyès
32.	Abísúgà	Born into a palace
33.	Abítoyè	Born to live with chieftaincy
34.	Abóriṣàdé	He that arrived with the (family) Òrìṣà, child born during the celebration of the Òrìṣà's festival
35.	Abóḍerìn	He that walked with hunter to arrive, child born during the hunter's festival
36.	Abóḍúnrìn	He that walked with the year, child born during the celebration of any annual festival
37.	Abóḍúnwá	Same as Abóḍúnrìn
38.	Abólárìn	He who walks in the company of honour just bestowed on family member
39.	Abósẹ̀dé	Arrived on the holy day of the family divinity, or nowadays, Sunday
40.	Abóyadé	Arrived with Ọya, child born during the formal worship of Ọya river divinity
41.	Àbọ̀ábá	Came back to meet at home. Child born during the absence of the father from home
42.	Àbọ̀wábá	The full phrase of the contracted Àbọ̀ábá
43.	Àbùdí ọrẹ	Inexhaustible gift
44.	Abúlùdé	He that arrived with the drum – born during drummer's annual festival
45.	Adáramọ́lá	He that is handsome, in addition to being honourable
46.	Adèagbo	The crown of the family clan, or crowd

	Name	Meaning and Circumstances
47.	Adéẹ̀yọ̀	The crown of the Ẹ̀yọ̀ masquerade worshipped in the family
48.	Adékóyẹni	One whose arrival dignifies us
49.	Àdèlé	Successor, he that will keep and run the house when the father is dead
50.	Adéníba	The crown has a father – first son of an Adé family
51.	Adéòjó	The crown (first son) of a man called Òjó
52.	Adéolú	The crown of Olú, the paramount chief, heir apparent
53.	Àdìmúlà	Holding on to him will bring wealth or make one rich
54.	Adíñléwá	Dialect variant of Adérinléwá – the crown walks home (here)
55.	Adú(máadán)	Glitteringly beautiful black (child)
56.	Àdùbí	He that we scrambled to bear as a child (not Ìgè)
57.	Adúlójú	The one with the black face
58.	Adùnọlá	The sweetness of honour
59.	Àdúràágbà	(My) prayers are effective
60.	Àdùwò	He who many relatives scramble to look after
61.	Áfikúyọ̀mí	There was death that could have made my enemies to ridicule me
62.	Afolúkẹ́	She who is to be pampered with the grandeur of Olú the paramount chief
63.	Afọlábí	One given birth to with affluence and honour
64.	Afọlágbadé	One who received the crown with honour
65.	Afọlákẹ́	She who is to be pampered with family, affluence and honour

	Name	Meaning and Circumstances
66.	Afọlálù	One who adds to honour
67.	Afọlámí	He who breathes with dignity – healthy child who breathes a little more slowly during the first week of life
68.	Afọlárànmí	He who infects me with honour, spreads honour to reach me
69.	Afọlárìn	He who walks in (at birth) with dignified honour – child born on schedule with easy labour and no complications
70.	Afọláyan	He who marches in (at birth) with dignified honour – child born after a very short, clean, uncomplicated labour
71.	Afọlọ́runṣọ́	We leave him under the protection of Ọlọ́run – God. A precious child who must survive at all costs.
72.	Àfọ̀njá	One of the totems of the Aláàfin literally the African bread fruit (áfọ̀n) drops from the tree (and falls on the head of Aláàfin's enemies or conspirators)
73.	Afùàpé	One who is perfect in character. A healthy but rather quiet child who feeds, sleeps, and defecates on schedule during the first week of life
74.	Afùwàpé	Fully spelt out name of Afùàpé
75.	Àgbálájọbí	Born with collective/communal efforts
76.	Àgbara	A contraction of "Àgbà – ara " – elderly body. Name given to a child born to an elderly father and/or by an elderly mother
77.	Àgbéjóka	To be carried and danced about with (see Àgbélúsì)
78.	Àgbéjoyè	To be carried and become chief

	Name	Meaning and Circumstances
79.	Àgbégbọlá	To be carried about and receive honour (see Àgbélúsì)
80.	Àgbélúsì	To be carried and become famous. Child born after very, very many years of doing everything possible to get a pregnancy, and his birth and being carried around will make the mother famous
81.	Àgbélúyì	Have prestige. (see Àgbélúsì)
82.	Àgbétúyì	Is prestigious (see Àgbélúsì)
83.	Àgbétùyìn	Child to be piggy-backed to comfort the back (first child after very many frustrating years of looking for a pregnancy)
84.	Àgbẹ́ẹ́sanmí	Farming has been good to me, has made me wealthy
85.	Àgbẹ́ẹ́sànwá	Farming has been good to us, has made me wealthy
86.	Àgbẹ́ẹ́sanwá	Language variant of Àgbẹ́ẹ́sànwá
87.	Agboọlá	Circle or flock of honour. Child born as son number four or higher
88.	Agbólúajé	A contraction of Agbólúwajé
89.	Agbólúwajé	He who makes Olú become rich in investments
90.	Agbọ́ládé	He who brings in honour (ọlá). A male child born after two or more female children in succession
91.	Àgbéjọba	To be carried and honoured like a king
92.	Agbọláhàn	He who exhibits honour (Ọlá). A language variant of Agbọ́ládé
93.	Áìíbínúọmọ	People do not get annoyed with the birth of a child
94.	Aílérù	A contracted form of Ayélérù, the world (people) is to be feared

	Name	Meaning and Circumstances
95.	Àjàgbé	Carried with a fight. Name given to the first child of a woman captured in war and married (also a pet-name)
96.	Àjàlá	He who survived a hard fight. Name given to a child born healthy after a labour complicated with cross-body presentation at first
97.	Ajé(dé)	Investment or Money has arrived. Shortened form of the name Àjede
98.	Àjede	Investment has arrived. Child born shortly after the father or mother arrived home from a very profitable day at the market, or first female child after many males
99.	Ajétúnmọbí	Profitable investment makes a child to be born again
100.	Ajíbábìí	He who wakes up to meet family members
101.	Ajíbádé	Wakes up to meet the crown. Name of male child in a royal family, or a family whose totem is the crown Adé
102.	Ajibájé	He who wakes up to meet money. Child born when profitable commercial ventures have just improved the parent's quality of life significantly
103.	Ajíbíkẹ́ẹ́	He/She who wakes in the morning to meet pampering. First child (usually) with the two grandmothers around to take care of him/her alongside the parents
104.	Ajíbódù	He who wakes up to meet Ifá of Ifá corpus
105.	Ajíbówú	He who wakes up to meet "owú", the very heavy iron mallet used by blacksmiths. Name given to a blacksmith's son if he would not be given an Ògún name, or in addition to the Ògún name
106.	Ajíbóyè	Wakes up to meet chieftaincy title. Name of a male child of a titled chief

	Name	Meaning and Circumstances
107.	Ajíbọ́lá	Wakes up to meet honour - Ọlá. Name given to a male or female child in a family whose totem is "Ọlá"
108.	Ajíbọ́sẹ̀	Wakes up to meet the holy day of the worship of the family Deity, child born in the early hours of the family Sabbath day
109.	Ajílóre	He who wakes up to have many relations (who render help)
110.	Ajíjọlá	He who wakes up to enjoy wealth
111.	Ajíléyẹ	Wakes up to possess dignity. Child born shortly after a befitting honour has been bestowed on his father or grandfather
112.	Ajímọ̀bí	Wakes up to know members of the extended family. Child born on the day that a traditional family meeting took place
113.	Àjíún	One who "bluffs" at being aroused from sleep
114.	Ajọ́sẹ̀	The worshipper, child born on the family Sabbath day
115.	Àjùmọ̀(bí)	The shortened form of Àjùmọ̀bí
116.	Àjùmọ̀bí	Jointly born. Child born to a man who has a lot of medicinal or financial help from his relatives before and/or during the pregnancy
117.	Àjùwọ̀n	Name given to males in Ọyọ́ royal family. Original Àjùwọ̀n was the brother of Aláàfin Ṣàngó
118.	Akéré(korò)	Small (and bitter). A child with significantly low weight at birth, but is nonetheless a very loud persistent crier
119.	Akérédolú	Small to become paramount. Child born with a significantly low weight into a family whose totem is Olú

	Name	Meaning and Circumstances
120.	Akéréle	Small and tough. Child born with a low weight but nonetheless behaving with bouncing health, cries and feeding
121.	Aládégbayé	The crowned one occupies/possesses the world
122.	Aládéjánà(ọlà)	The crowned one enters the road to wealth
123.	Aládéjẹbí	The crowned one assembles/builds the family
124.	Aládéèjẹ̀bi	The crowned one is not guilty/wrong in the existing quarrel. Child born after an easy uncomplicated labour as proof of innocence in an existing big family quarrel
125.	Aládéèkọmọ	The crowned one is always surrounded with children, does not reject children
126.	Alàdémọ̀mí	The crowned one knows me. First male child born to a man married to a woman from an "Adé" family
127.	Aládéṣawẹ̀	The crowned one is cleansed of infertility
128.	Aládéṣèlú	It is the crowned one who runs the town
129.	Àlàfúnkintodòbọ̀	The white cloth comes back immaculate white from the river (the birth of this male child spotlights the family specially)
130.	Alàgbàoṣó	The elderly wizard/seer/wise. Child who at birth had one or more features of the elderly (like strands of gray hair) in an "oṣó" family.
131.	Alálàádé	The owner of the immaculate white cloth (àlà) has arrived
132.	Aláwodé	The owner of the family cult has arrived. Child born into a named cult family or during the celebration of the family cult festival
133.	Aláyàn-ándé	The owner of "àyàn", the totem of vocational drummers has arrived. First son born into a drummer's family

	Name	Meaning and Circumstances
134.	Alẹ́dá.re	The evening has judged (me) innocent (of impotence). First child of a middle-aged or elderly man who has been married for many years without a child
135.	Alẹ́sànmí	The evening profits me. Child born to an old man, who may or may not have had any child before
136.	Aófiyèbí	The cult gives birth to this with great understanding
137.	Àràbambí	Dexterous dancing has helped me to bear this child. An exclusive Òǹdó name for a child born to the family of dexterous dancers during Ògún festival
138.	Àrágbayé	Wonders occupy life (the world)
139.	Àràlọla	Novelty is honour. Dexterous dancing during Ògún festival is honour
140.	Arámìídé	My relative has arrived. First child of (usually) an only child, or a person who has settled very far from his parents' town
141.	Aránmọláté	One who sends a child to buy a traditional umbrella (áté) to protect one from rain. Child born when it was threatening to rain heavily.
142.	Arárọ̀mí	My body is relaxed. Child born after many years' efforts to have a pregnancy
143.	Àránsíọlá	Honour specially sent to me. Child born from an unexpected marriage or unexpected pregnancy.
144.	Àràáwọlé	Novelty enters the house. First child born to a family of Òǹdó's unique dexterous dancing during Ògún festival.
145.	Aráwọmọ	Relations are enough to bring up a child (whose mother died at birth)
146.	Àrẹtáyọ̀	The Àrẹ title is worth being joyous about

	Name	Meaning and Circumstances
147.	Àrẹtọ́lá	The leader's title is as valuable as honour
148.	Aríbamíkàn	One who gives a sign of relief on sighting his father
149.	Aríbisálà	One who finds a place to run to for safety. Child born away from parents' hometown where mother moved to for safe delivery
150.	Arídẹgbé	He who finds a brass to lift/possess. Child born to a brass-smith family, when the father or grandfather was actively engaged in brass works in his workshop
151.	Aríyìíbí	We found this specially to give birth to
152.	Aríyìíkẹ́	We have got this one to pamper. Child born shortly after the death of another
153.	Àríyọ̀	One whose being sighted gladdens one's heart. Child anxiously expected to be male, and turns out so.
154.	Arógundádé	One who puts on crown on sighting an opposing army. Male child born after a hotly contested bid to marry his mother, or after a contest over the pregnancy
155.	Arómirẹ́	Child who from birth enjoys being bathed; does not cry when being washed
156.	Atẹ́wọ́gboyè	Open palms to receive chieftaincy title. Child born in Oyè family, who kept his palms unusually open during the first week of life
157.	Atiládé	We have possessed a crown. First child so named by his/her father or grandfather
158.	Atólágbé	Strong enough to carry honour (Ọlá). An Ọlá – family child whose inactivity during the first few days of life caused some anxiety but the parents reassured themselves with this name, that he will survive

	Name	Meaning and Circumstances
159.	Àwẹ̀dá	Medicinal/fertility bath cleans (me) up, is efficacious
160.	Atóyèbí	Enough for Oyè to have as a child. An Oyè child with very low weight
161.	Àwála	Child whose parents became rich or had a lead to wealth in the process of searching for his/her pregnancy
162.	Awẹ́	A child with very low birth-weight
163.	Àwùjọọlá	Congregation of honour. Child born into an family that is already got many children
164.	Ayédọgbọ́n	Life now depends on cunning wisdom
165.	Ayégbọ́	The world hears of this momentous birth
166.	Ayéníbá	The world has disappointment. Child born to a father who was then experiencing significant let-downs from people
167.	Ayenúmẹ̀lọ	The world (life) has to be taken easy. Child born when a highly coincidental tragedy occurred to somebody else, and it became a warning not to be in physical combat with anybody, no matter the provocation
168.	Ayéṣemínínkan	The world has afflicted me. Child born to a father in distress/trouble that he believed was caused by enemies
169.	Ayéètúyọ̀mí	People have no cause to ridicule me, or gloat at my misfortune
170.	Ayéyí	The world has turned. Male child born after many females
171.	Babalọlá	Father is honour. Child born to a man who was enjoying significant social deference because of his father
172.	Babaríñsá	Father saw me and ran. Child whose father died during the first week of its birth

	Name	Meaning and Circumstances
173.	Babtọ́pẹ́	Father is enough to be grateful for. Child born to a man whose father funded his marriage or otherwise gave significant support for the child's arrival
174.	Bámgbálà	Help me carry white cloth - . First son born into the family of the worshippers of Ọbàtálá /Òrìṣà - oko, who do not want to give a name to the child.
175.	Bídèmí	Born waiting for me. Child born when the father was away on a long trip, in some areas, the trip may last many years.
176.	Bílésanmí	If the home is satisfying to me that is sweeter than (chieftaincy title). Child born when the father is experiencing some disappointments.
177.	Bọ́látitó	Bọ́lá is enough. Last born of three or four children whose names start with Bọ́lá.
178.	Bọ́lọ́rundúró	Stand with God. Child born to a father who believes experientially that he has no helper except God.
179.	Dáramọ́lá	Handsome in addition to family honour
180.	Èébúdọlá	Insults became honour. Child born to a woman who for very many years could not get pregnant and was therefore being insulted by the husband and/or other wives who were mothers in the family
181.	Èédú	Charcoal. Child with exceptionally black complexion.
182.	Èjìadé	The second crown
183.	Èènúyọ̀	Not enough to be glad for. Child born when deaths of many young people occurred in the family, or the immediate social environment in an Ìjẹ̀bú town
184.	Èésúọlá	Pool of honour. Child born into a happy-go-lucky family of many children

	Name	Meaning and Circumstances
185.	Elégbè	The owner of the farmstead or farm settlement first son
186.	Elégbèédé	A staunch supporter has arrived. First child born to a man who believes that he was ill-treated because he had no children to fight his cause. Birth of this child consoles and gives hope that such ill-treatment would not occur in future
187.	Erìkìtọ́lá / Erìgìtọ́lá	Possession of molar-teeth to do one's chewing (to solve one's problem by oneself) is as good as honour.
188.	Èsúrúoṣó	Exceptionally light-complexioned child born into an Oṣó family
189.	Èsúrúọlá	Uncommon honour, special blessing
190.	Èpémòólú	The curse did not affect Olú. Child born after a bitter conflict that involved cursing
191.	Ewéjẹ́	The leaf agreed, the medicine worked. Child whose pregnancy came as a result of medicine taken or sacrifices made
192.	Ewéjúya	Leaf is possible to tear. Child whose pregnancy occurred as a result of the mother taking some herbal medicine
193.	Éwùmí	I just love him/her. The child whose birth has been anxiously awaited by most probably the grandfather
194.	Èyítáyọ̀	This is worthy of joy
195.	Èyítọlá	This is worthy of honours, it is as good as honour
196.	Èyítọ́láámí	This is enough for honour to continue breathing. A child whose birth gave succor to an otherwise distressed family
197.	Èbùn	Gift (of God)

	Name	Meaning and Circumstances
198.	Ẹbùnolúwa	Gift of the Lord, Male or female child from an unexpected pregnancy or child of undesired gender
199.	Èérínoṣó	Child born into an Oṣó family that already has many children
200.	Ẹgbẹ́ẹ̀yẹ	Dignifying comrades. Child born to join many other children of dignity in the family.
201.	Ẹgbẹ́olú	Comrades of Olú. Child born in a family of many Olús before him/her
202.	Ẹjọ́ọ̀fòdọ́mi	The quarrel or court-case did not reach me. Child born when the father or grandfather was luckily excluded from a raging village/town conflict
203.	Ẹkúndayọ̀	Tears became joy. Child born very shortly after a family tragedy or loss, or after many years search for a pregnancy
204.	Ẹ̀mílójù	Life is most important. Child born during or shortly after a huge financial or property loss by the father or mother
205.	Ẹ̀míọlá	The breath of honour. Female child who was unusually low-breathing, quiet-crying an inactive during the first week of life (at least)
206.	Ẹniitàn	A person of history. Child born (or found to be named) under extremely tragic or trying circumstances that were not conducive to the child's survival
207.	Ẹnímọ̀la(òsí)	Nobody knows tomorrow
208.	Ẹnitáànwá	Person we have been searching for. First or any child whose pregnancy occurred after a "search" of many years
209.	Èríìfẹ́	Evidence of love. Child of a normally unexpected match

	Name	Meaning and Circumstances
210.	Ẹ̀san	Compensation or vengeance. Child born and seen by parents as compensation for the loss/death of another child
211.	Èsángbẹ̀dọ̀	Vengeance requires caution. Child born to a father who wants to take vengeance discreetly or has just seen vengeance boomerang on somebody else
212.	Ẹ̀sán-júùgbà	Vengeance is impossible. Child born to a man who had recently been grievously hurt by someone who is too close or loved to be hurt back
213.	Ẹ̀yìnlánwò	It is posterity we are looking at to tamper our reaction
214.	Fáàdayọ̀mí	The Ifá deity has not allowed my enemies to gloat over my misfortune
215.	Farayọ́la	Rub your body on honour. Child born to a father who has recently been elevated to a higher social status
216.	Fèyíṣẹ̀tàn	Make history out of this
217.	Fìjàbí	Born with a quarrel/fight. Child whose pregnancy occurred as the result of reconciliation after a quarrel between the parents, or as part of the quarrel
218.	Folówóṣẹlé	Introduce the rich into the house. Child whose family was visited unexpectedly, and given a lot of money by a "rich" man during the first week of the child's life.
219.	Fọláṣadé	Make honour a crown. Be proud to be born into an ọlá family
220.	Fọláwẹwọ́	Wash hands with honour. There is so much honour in the family that you can clean your hands with it
221.	Fọláwíyọ́	A language variant of Fọláwẹwọ́

	Name	Meaning and Circumstances
222.	Fólórunṣó	Left under the protection and guard of God. A precious child who must survive at all costs
223.	Gbádégẹ̀sin	Put the crown on horseback. Child born into an adé family at the time when the father has just been vindicated on an issue
224.	Gbogboadé	As assemblance of all crowns
225.	Gbólúwaga	Lift the Lord high. Name given in praise of God for the child's safe arrival. The name is Christianity-tinted
226.	Gbọ́ládé	Bring honour here. See Agbọ́ládé
227.	Gbọ́láhàn	Exhibit honour. See Agbọ́láhàn
228.	Gbọ́tibaba	Listen to and obey your father (Father's advice works well)
229.	Ìbídún(únní)	Pedigree is sweet (to have). Child born with unusually active support (medicinally or financially) of the extended family
230.	Ìbídùnmóyè	Good pedigree is pleasurably compatible with chieftaincy title
231.	Ìbùkún(olú)	Blessing (of God). Literally, "an addition" to the family from (God)
232.	Ìbùkúnọlá	Addition to honour. Child who arrived ordinarily as an addition to many older children
233.	Ìdóníbóyè	Ìdó (a town) is where to meet chieftaincy title.
234.	Ìfẹolú	The love of the paramount chief. Nowadays, the love of God. Child born by a woman whose marriage to her husband was with the active support of the paramount chief
235.	Ìfẹ́túgà	Love is as valuable as palace
236.	Ìfẹ́yinwá	Love praises us. Child born to a couple who kept their marriage vows despite a fairly long involuntary delay in the child's pregnancy

	Name	Meaning and Circumstances
237.	Ìgbẹ́kẹ̀lé	Hope
238.	Ìgèodù	A breech child born into an Odù family (see Àmútọ̀runwá names)
239.	Ìjàdùọlá	Honour that was scrambled for. Child born from a pregnancy whose ownership was contested by two men, or born by a woman whose hand in marriage was sought by many men
240.	Ìjàgbúyìró	Quarrel sustained dignity. Child born when a man has just been involved in a conflict in which he did not compromise his dignity
241.	Ìjálànà	Quarrel cleared the way. Child born from a pregnancy that occurred as a result of a big quarrel or separation that the man had with another wife
242.	Ìjàámákinwá	Quarrel brought the brave or the warrior. Child from a pregnancy immediately after settling a family quarrel
243.	Ìkẹ́olú	The pampering of Olú. Female first child of a man whose wife was given him free or relatively cheaply by the paramount chief. Nowadays, it means the pampering of God.
244.	Ìkọ̀ọ́túndé	The messenger (of the family divinity) has come again. Child born with a birth-mark of the divinity anointed
245.	Ikúmógunníyì	Death gives dignity to warfare. Child born at a time a loved one has just died in war
246.	Ikúmọ́mọníṣẹ́	Death makes a child have a vocation. Philosophical warning that every person should have a job and not depend on rich parents who may die at any time
247.	Ikúòmọlá	Death did not take honour away. Consolatory name given to a child born at the time of the death of a beloved one

	Name	Meaning and Circumstances
248.	Ikúpẹlẹ́yẹ	Death has killed the person with dignity. Child born shortly after the death of a highly respected family member or benefactor
249.	Ikú.pọlátán	Death did not kill all honour. Child born and named as an assurance that honour still remains despite the recent multiple deaths in the family
250.	Ikúpọláti	Death failed to kill all honour. An assertive verdict of family survival. Child born shortly after multiple deaths in the family
251.	Ikúyájẹ̀ṣín	Death is faster/easier to bear than ridicule. A maxim that prescribes suicide instead of being a cause of ridicule to family honour. Child born when such a ridicule was going on publicly to a family member
252.	Ilémbóyè	I met chieftaincy title at home. Child born shortly after the father or grandfather has just been given a title or just revived an old family title
253.	Ilémobáyọ̀	Met joy at home. Child born during or shortly after a joyous celebration in the family
254.	Ìlériolúwa	The promise of the Lord (God). Child whose birth was seen as a fulfillment of God's promise through religious faith or pronouncement
255.	Ilésanmí	The house satisfies me. A pronouncement of contentment with one's lot, without any chieftaincy title. Child born shortly after a social disappointment
256.	Ìmọlẹ́yìn	Knowledge after the incident, or knowledge has a back (consequences). A modern name to toast the honour of university graduation of a family member at the time this child was born
257.	Ìpàdéọlá	The meeting of honour. Child born when a "meeting of minds" turned out to be great benefit to the family
258.	Ìrètí	Hope. A contraction of Ìrètíọlá

	Name	Meaning and Circumstances
259.	Ìrètíọlá	Hope for honour. Child born as a first child or first female, routinely expected or hoped for
260.	Ìrọ̀rùn	Ease/Comfort. Child born with all-round ease and very little anxiety in the family, medically especially
261.	Ìṣíjọlà	The opening (first child) is more than wealth
262.	Ìtẹolúwakìíṣí	The throne of God never moves. Child born as a result of much prayers and supplication and named to reaffirm faith in God
263.	Ìtíolú	Bundle of Olú. Name given to a child in an Olú family where there has been at least five children before or name given to the last child in a multiple birth
264.	Ìtùnù	Consolation. Child born shortly after a tragic loss of life and or property in the family
265.	Ìwàájọmọ	(Good) character assembles children (causes one to have many children)
266.	Ìwàlẹ̀yẹ	Character is dignity. Child born at a time that the father or mother was savouring the reward of good behavior in the society
267.	Ìwásànmí	Character is rewarding to me. Child born when the father or grandfather (who gave the name) is savouring the reward of some good behavior
268.	Ìyàndá	The famine stops. Male child after a long unexpected cease of pregnancies in two or more wives
269.	Ìyébùsọ́lá	This one adds to honour (Ìjẹ̀ṣà)
270.	Iyìọlá	The prestige of honour. Child whose birth added more prestige to the ọlá family
271.	Jọláadé	Revel in the honour of the crown. Female child born by a woman from an Adé family

	Name	Meaning and Circumstances
272.	Káfidiyà	Let us use it (the child) as compensation for our unjustified punishment or hard times. Child born during or shortly after hard times being experienced by the parents
273.	Kẹ́kẹ́loyè	Chieftaincy is as beautifying as the Òwu kẹ́kẹ́ facial marks
274.	Kíkẹ́lọlá	Honour is to be pampered. Female child born into an ọlá family, probably after two or more male children
275.	Kíkẹ́lọmọ	The child is for pampering. Female child born into a non-totem family, probably after two or more male children
276.	Kòfowórọlá	Did not use money to buy honour. Female child born into an ọlá family that is affluent. Name to show that the ọlá has always been there
277.	Kòríbamọ̀	Did not see a father to know. Child born after the death of his/her father
278.	Kòséèbínú(ayé)	The world (people) is not angry with me
279.	Kọ́léoṣó	Build the house of the wizard/seer. First male child born to an Oṣó family
280.	Kúboyè	Death overwhelms the joy of chieftaincy
281.	Kúfoníyì	Death spared (jumped over) the prestigious one. Child born at a time that a precious elderly family member has just recovered from a life threatening illness
282.	Kúùjẹ́mbọ́là	Death did not allow me to meet wealth. Child born shortly after the death of a wealthy and generous man in the family
283.	Kúmòólú	Death has not taken Olú, male child born when the head of the family or the king has just died without a heir

	Name	Meaning and Circumstances
284.	Kúmúyi	Death has taken prestige (away). Child born when a "star" in the family has just died, and caused sadness
285.	Kúpo	shortened form of Kúpolúyì
286.	Kúpolúyì	Death has killed the owner of prestige. Child born when a family "star" or benefactor has just died (Ìjẹ̀ṣa)
287.	Kúponíyì	the literary Yorùbá language of Kúpolúyì
288.	Kúùrunmí	Death has not exterminated me. Child born when many able-bodied family members were dying in quick succession or epidemic, and the birth of this child is an indication of hope of family survival
289.	Kúrunmí	Death has exterminated me. Child born when many (all) able-bodied men in the family died in such quick succession that the father or grandfather of the child had lost hope of family continuity
290.	Kúùyẹ̀	Death does not change. A shortened form of Kúùyẹ̀bí
291.	Kúùyẹ̀bí	Death does not change family relationships. Child born when the family has experienced many deaths in quick succession and the giver of this name wished that he could belong to a luckier family, but alas!
292.	(A)Ládégbùwà	The crowned one receives character (of honour). First male child born into an Adé family
293.	(A)Ládéjọbi	Crowned ones gave birth to this child together. Child born by a woman from an Adé family married to a man from an Adé family
294.	(Ọ)Láńdé	My honour has arrived. First child or first male born in any family, not necessarily an Olá family

	Name	Meaning and Circumstances
295.	(Ọ)Láńlẹ́gẹ́	My honour is delicate. Male child born prematurely and or with very low weight and delicate features at birth to an Olá family
296.	(Ọ)Láòṣe(bìkan)	Honour is not restricted to only one place. Child born shortly after the news of birth by another member of the family, or the news of an honour being bestowed on another member of the extended family
297.	(Ó)Lìjàdù	Has to be scrambled for. Child born to a man who competed actively with other men for the hand of his wife in marriage
298.	(O) Lípẹ̀ẹ́dé	The consoler/comforter has arrived. Child born during a sad occurrence in the family
299.	Májìyàgbé	Do not suffer punishment or ill-treatment in vain birth of the child seen as compensation
300.	Makàn-án-júọlá	Do not be in a hurry for honour. Child born when one or more people on the fast lane of life has just died painfully or when patience has just paid off for a family member
301.	Máyọ̀mí	Do not gloat over my misfortune or tribulations
302.	Méègbọwọn	I did not listen to them (bad advisers or detractors)
303.	Mémùwùawọn	I do not know their character. Child born to a father who has just been let down in a big way by relatives
304.	Méèṣayétẹ̀	I did not step on the wrong side of the world. Child whose birth reassures the father that his marriage was proper and he did not offend anyone
305.	Métílélùú	Put ear to the town (listen to people). Child born to a king or politically powerful person who has just benefited from grapevine information
306.	Mobẹ̀rẹ̀ọlé	I just started honour. First child in an Olá family

	Name	Meaning and Circumstances
307.	Mobólurìn	I walked with. Child born during the coronation of the king
308.	Mobólají	I woke up alongside honour. First child in any family can be so named, especially if born during the early hours of the day
309.	Modúpẹ́	I thank (God)
310.	Mofadékẹ́	I use the crown to pet. Child born into an Adé family shortly after the coronation of the father or a close family relation
311.	Mofògúnkẹ́	I use the divinity of iron to pamper. Child born during or shortly after the Ògún festival
312.	Mofolúkẹ́	I use Olú to pamper. Child born when father or grandfather has just been honoured or shown special favours by the king. Nowadays, Olú could be the shortened form of Olúwa (Lord God)
313.	Mofolúwaṣọ́	I put under the protection of God. Child born to a father who had mysteriously lost another child not long ago
314.	Mojísọlá	I wake into honour. Child whose birth was known to the father very early in the morning
315.	Mojoyin	I eat honey. Shortened form of Mojoyinọlá - enjoy marrying into an ọlá family. First female child after marriage so named by father
316.	Moládé	I have a crown. first child may be so named by its father
317.	Molólúwa	I have the Lord, God. Child born when "help of the helpless" has just manifested in the father's life or family circumstances
318.	Monẹ́bí	I have family. First child to a father who felt his extended family has not been supportive, and the child was his own personal family
319.	Monílọlá	I now have my share of honour

	Name	Meaning and Circumstances
320.	Mopélọlá	I am complete in honour. Female child born after one or more males. Completion of honour is when one has both male and female children
321.	Morádèún	I saw the crown and assumed airs or become pompous. Child in Adé family with usually heavy weight and "pompous behavior at birth"
322.	Morákinyọ̀	I saw the brave and became joyous. First male child in an Akin family that has had one or more females before
323.	Moráyọ̀	I see joy. Name given a child usually by a grandparent whose family life in the recent past has been unusually dull
324.	Morẹnikéji	I have seen a person to be my second. First female child born to a young couple living far away from home
325.	Moróundíyà	I have found/possessed something to compensate me for the undeserved punishment or ill-treatment that I had
326.	Moróunfólú	I have seen something to give Olú. Male child that could be presented to the king for fighting in future wars. Nowadays, it means I have seen something to give God, and completed as "Thanks"
327.	Moróunkéjì	A Yorùbé dialect variant of Morẹnikéji
328.	Moróunmúbọ̀	I have seen something to bring back. Child born to a couple that is resident very far away from home
329.	Morọláwún	I saw honour and assumed airs or became pompous. Child in ọlá family, heavy weight at birth, and "pompous" behavior during the first week of life
330.	Morọláyọ̀	I see honour and become joyous/happy

	Name	Meaning and Circumstances
331.	Mosádolú	I escaped to Olú as my refuge. Child born to a father who begged for the king's intervention before he was allowed to marry his wife
332.	Mosádogun	I escaped to the war as refuge. Child born to a father who literally joined the army to escape some punishment or his creditors, whom he satisfied after the war
333.	Mosúnmọ́lá	I move near to honour. Child born by a plebeian father and a mother from an ọlá family, or otherwise notable family
334.	Moṣebọ́látán	I thought honour was finished. Child born so many years after the last one that the woman was thought to be menopausal
335.	Motọ́lá	I am as precious as honour
336.	Motúnráyọ́	I have seen joy again. Child born shortly after uncle or aunt died and grandfather proclaimed himself seeing joy again
337.	Moyọ̀sóore	I am joyous at the kindness (of God). Child born without expected medical complications or any other anxieties
338.	Mọladé	The child is one's crown
339.	Òfòólùwá	A great loss has hit us. Child whose mother died during labour or during the first week of the child's life, or whose family suffered one other tragic loss
340.	Ògúuwá	The divinity of iron of the future. First male child expected to lead in the family worship of the divinity in future
341.	Ògún-un-wá	Literary Yorùbá variant of Ògúuwá
342.	Ogbèéṣetuyì	Èjìogbè, the primus Odù in Ifá has done a prestigious thing

	Name	Meaning and Circumstances
343.	Ojúgbélẹ̀	The eye stops roving (stays on the ground). Child born to a man who had been childless for many years even after trying for pregnancy with at least three women. Child whose birth brings relief from anxieties
344.	Ojúmiírí	My eye saw (a lot of suffering). Child born shortly after some harrowing experiences by the father
345.	Ojúọlé	The face of honour
346.	Ojúọlápé	The faces of honour are complete
347.	Ojúrí	The eye saw (a lot of suffering). Same as Ojúmiírí
348.	Ojútaláyọ̀	The joyous ones (at the misfortune) are shamed. Child born to a father who had just overcome some misfortune which he believed some people were gloating over
349.	Okunlọlá	My honour is plentiful as the sea
350.	Òkunmotibọ̀	The sea is where I have come from. Child born while the parents were across waters far away from home. One who comes to complete family titles and honours
351.	Olíkóyè	One who comes to complete family titles and honours
352.	Olíyìídè	The prestigious one has arrived
353.	Ológùn-únrìndé	The owner (worshipper) of the divinity of iron has arrived walking. First male child of a blacksmith, or son born into an Ògún family during the annual festival
354.	Ológundé	The warrior has arrived. First son born to a warrior family, or diviner predicated before birth to grow up to be a warrior in a non-warrior family

	Name	Meaning and Circumstances
355.	Olófundúdú	The black warrior. Unusually pitch black, child born into a warrior family, or diviner predicated before birth to be a warrior in a non-warrior family
356.	Olókodé	The owner on the farm (landlord) has come
357.	Olókùúdé	the owner of the corpse had come. Not a name given at birth. It was a situational appellate given to the first son of a very famous dead man, when he (the son) arrived home for the father's burial. It became a surname through the English nuclear naming system
358.	Olóríajé	The one destined to be lucky in commerce
359.	Olórìṣàádé	The worshipper of the deity has come. Child born during the annual festival of the family god/goddess
360.	Olóròódé	The owner (worshipper) of Orò (the curfew insignia) has come. Male child born into an Orò worshipping family, especially during the festival
361.	Olówóyẹyè	The rich fits a chieftaincy title. Child born to a rich man who had just had a chieftaincy title and very many chiefs came to greet him because of his wealth
362.	Ológunwá	The warrior comes in (see Ológundé)
363.	Olóyèédé	The titled chief has come. Heir apparent born to a titled chief
364.	Olódùúdé	The owner of Odù (Ifá corpus) has arrived. Child born into an Ifá worshipping family or born exactly according to a specific odù that appeared on the diviner's board about him, before his birth
365.	Olówúdé	The owner of the blacksmith's hammer has arrived
366.	Olówudé	the king of Òwu has arrived as heir apparent or reincarnated

	Name	Meaning and Circumstances
367.	Olúmilúà	My Lord has character. Child born as prayed for, in reference to the occurrence of the pregnancy, complications at birth, or the child being male
368.	Olúmodéjì	O Lord, I have become two. First child born to a young couple, probably resident very far away from home
369.	Olúọmọ	The paramount child. Son born after many daughters
370.	Olúodò	The lord of the river. First daughter born to an Omi family, and divined before birth to be a leading worshipper of the deity
371.	Olúwafẹ́mi	The Lord (God) loves me. Child born as expected easily, and given this name to express belief in God's love
372.	Olúwamáyọ̀kún	The Lord makes joy to be full. Child born by a mother who recovered from some serious anxiety, that created complications during labour, or during the first week of giving birth
373.	Olúwambẹ	God is the ultimate succor
374.	Ómámẹ̀	He took the distinguishing mark. Child born with birth-mark, he/she had been divined to have if he/she were the expected reincarnation
375.	Oníbíìyọ̀	The owner of (supportive) pedigree rejoices. Child born to parents who had a lot of support from their relatives
376.	Onibòkun	The person who arrived from the sea/ocean. Child born to Ìjẹ̀ṣà across water far away from home
377.	Onífádé	The owner of the Ifá oracle or the worshipper of the Ifá oracle has arrived. First son born to an Ifá diviner or his close relation

	Name	Meaning and Circumstances
378.	Onigbìn-in-dé	The owner of "ìgbìn" a special drum has arrived. First son born to the family that specializes in making the "ìgbìn" drum, and beating the drum at appropriate festivals
379.	Òníkẹ̀ẹ̀kù	People who will pamper (children) still remain. Female child born shortly after the death of a loving grandmother or aunt
380.	Oníkẹ̀ẹ́pé	People who will pamper (children) are all present. Female child whose birth brought an assembling of both grandmothers and aunties to pamper her
381.	Onípẹ̀ẹ́dé	The comforter/consoler has come
382.	Oníyẹléjù	The one who befits the house most (long expected male child after many females)
383.	Oníyìídé	The possessor of prestige has arrived. Child whose pregnancy coincided with an exceptionally prestigious occurrence in the family
384.	Oore-Olúwa	The kindness of the Lord (God)
385.	Oore-ọ̀fẹ́	Free kindness. Grace (of God). Male or female child of highly Christianly religious family
386.	Òótọ́jàre	Truth triumphs
387.	Ọ̀pópóọlá	The road to honour. First male child after one or more females
388.	Oríadé	The head of the crown. First male child in a young Adé family
389.	Oríjà (joògùn)	A person's head fights (for him) more than medicine or psychic power. Child born when one's head (providence) has just fought one's cause against powerful odds
390.	Orílawo	One's head is his protective occult
391.	Orímaládé	The head knows the person who will have a crown. An affirmation of the supremacy of providence (fate)

	Name	Meaning and Circumstances
392.	Orímolóyè	The head knows the person who will have a chieftaincy title. An affirmation of the supremacy of providence (fate) in human affairs
393.	Orímóògùnjẹ́	The head made the medicine to be efficacious. Child born when the father or grandfather needed to ascribe a unique success he experienced shortly before the birth of the child to his "head" (fate)
394.	Orímọ́ládé	The head brought honour to arrive. Child's father attributes the safe arrival of the child to his (father's) head (fate)
395.	Oríọlá	The head of honour. Child with an unusually big head at birth
396.	Òrìṣàádọta	The divinity has become granite (unconquerable). Child born safely after anxious ante-natal or labour experiences that caused the invocation of the Òrìṣà to fight all evil forces causing the troubles
397.	Orúkọfikàyọ̀n	Name makes counting and identification of people easy. Child born shortly after the father or grandfather has just been vindicated in a very serious case of mistaken identity
398.	Orùúyẹ̀lú	The sacrifice made in the water-pot benefits the town
399.	Òsùn-ún-dèé	The Ifá divine power ties this child down (with us)
400.	Òtítọ́jù	Truth is best. Child born at a time that truth has just prevailed in a serious conflict in which the father was involved
401.	Owóbámirìn	Money walked with me. Child born at a time of financial windfall for the family
402.	Owólabí	It is money we gave birth to. Child born after a very medically expensive pregnancy, and or born premature, a situation that will be costly

	Name	Meaning and Circumstances
403.	Owóṣeéní	Money can be had. Child born to a father who had a first-in-life financial break through
404.	Owóòtọ́mọ	Money is not as precious as a child. Child whose birth was seen as being worth all the expenses which depleted the family resources significantly
405.	Owúlólàwá	Jealousy stopped our fighting each other. Child born to a father who had thought of divorcing a wife, but got back to her when he saw that men of higher social status were courting her and he became jealous
406.	Oyèélẹ́gbin	Chieftaincy title has insults. Child born to a father who feels that having a chieftaincy title is demeaning
407.	Oyíndàmọ́lá	Honey poured into honour. First female child after one or more males
408.	Oyinloyè	Honey is chieftaincy title. Child born by a father who is enjoying the award
409.	Oyinlọlá	Honey is honour. First female child whose birth is seen as a great honour by the parents
410.	Oyinọlá	The honey of honour. First female child born into an Ọlá family
411.	Oyínsàn	Honey is good
412.	Ọbasá	The king (small pox) runs away. Child born when either of the parents, grandparents or older children has just recovered from an infection of small pox
413.	Ọdúnarò	The year of wailing. Child born in a year of great tribulations or sadness for the family
414.	Ọdúnayọ	The year of joy. Child born in a year of many joys like marriages, births, university graduation, promotion, house warming, etc.
415.	Ọdúnewu	The year of perils or dangers. Child born during a year of narrow misses, or survived accidents by prominent members of the family

	Name	Meaning and Circumstances
416.	Odúnjọ	The year assembled. Child born during a well-enjoyed annual festival
417.	Odún-ùn-jọ	The year did not assemble. Child born during an annual festival that could not be properly celebrated because of a tragic event or some deprivations
418.	Odúnsì	The year/festival does not cease, despite some unfavourable occurrences
419.	Odún-ùsì	The year of being famous. Child born in a year something happened to make the family famous
420.	Odún-ùjà	The year of a fight. Child born in the year that a war broke out or took place to involve the father of the child
421.	Odún-ùn-tàn	Year of history. Child born during a year of very important occurrences in the family
422.	Ògásọdé	The master emerges/has arrived. First male child after many females
423.	Ogbọ́nyọmí	Wisdom saved me
424.	Ojọ́lọ̀la	Tomorrow (posterity) is an important day. Child named to affirm that the future holds unknown mysteries
425.	Okánlàwọ́n	One different from them. First male child after many females
426.	Oláẹgbẹ́	The honour of the age group, or any other social group. Child born with the active support of comrades, probably in finding and marrying the wife
427.	Oláifá	The honour (help) of Ifá. Child whose pregnancy occurred as a result of consultation of Ifá and prescribed sacrifices
428.	Oláìyá	The honour (help) of mother, who either funded the marriage or otherwise gave active support for the child to be born to her son

	Name	Meaning and Circumstances
429.	Ọlámìòkúgbé	My Ọlá did not die without recompense, did not die in vain
430.	Ọláńbíwọnnínú	(My) honour (well-being) is annoying them. Child born during or shortly after the father was involved in a conflict in which he believed his opponents were just envious of him
431.	Ọláńbíwọnnú	The contracted form of Ọláńbíwọnnínú
432.	Ọláolú	The help of the king. Nowadays, is shortened form of Olúwa
433.	Ọláolúwa	The help of Ọláolúwa (God). Child born effortlessly and into such happy environment attributed mainly to an act of God
434.	Ọláoore	The reward of being kind. Child born in circumstances where the father, mother or close relation got help from a person(s) he had been kind to long ago
435.	Ọláọmọ	The largesse from an adult child
436.	Ọláọpá	The help of (drum) stick. Child born in a drumming family that gives credit for its good fortune to the vocation
437.	Ọláọrẹ	The help of a friend. Child born to a man who had the active support of a friend in finding the wife, funding the wedding or paying medical bills at birth
438.	Ọlọ́fin	The primogenitor of the Yorùbá race. it is the subject of the sentence as in the next four names below, but usage has cut off the predicate.
439.	Ọlọ́finbọ́ba	Ọlọ́fin gives birth to a king. First male child in an Ọlọ́fin worshipping family. (Ọlọ́fin is not universally worshipped in Yorùbá land)
440.	Ọlọ́fin-ínmọ̀yìn	The Supreme deity (Ọlọ́fin) knows/appreciates praise

	Name	Meaning and Circumstances
441.	Ọlọ́finíntilà	Ọlọ́fin has become wealthy
442.	Ọlọ́finnákin	Ọlọ́fin has courage. Ọlọ́fin has male children to give to an Akin family, after sacrifices were made to it
443.	Ọlọ́jẹ̀ẹ́dé	An ancestor-worshipper has arrived. Male child born into an Egúngún family, or predicted before pregnancy to be an ancestor-worshipper and born into non- Egúngún family
444.	Ọlọ́ládé	The honourable has arrived. Child born when a very special and significant honour has recently been bestowed on the family or father
445.	Ọlọ́mọọ́doṣi	One who has a child or children becomes a shrine. Child named to proclaim the sanctity of parenthood
446.	Ọlọ́mọọ́dòṣù	One who has a child or children initiates a perennial mound
447.	Ọlọ́mọọ́jọbí	Parents assemble/build families, or those who have children breed together. Child born to a family where on both father and mother's families children are many
448.	Ọlọ́mọlárá	A person who has children has relatives
449.	Ọlọ́mọlẹ́yìn	One who has a child or children has backbone. Child named to assert that parenthood is societal backbone
450.	Ọlọ́mọọ́lá	One who has a child or children is wealthy. Child named to assert the "wealth" of being a parent
451.	Ọlọ́mọpé	He/She who has a child or children is complete
452.	Ọlọ́nilúà	Person who has relatives has good fate. Child born with active support of relatives
453.	Ọlọ́runfẹ́mi	God loves me. Child born with no complications to a Christianly religious family
454.	Ọlọ́ṣundé	The worshipper of Ọ̀ṣun divinity has arrived

	Name	Meaning and Circumstances
455.	Ọmọlaṣọ	The child is clothes (to cover social nakedness). Child named to extol parenthood in the presence of poverty
456.	Ọmọyájowó	The child is more precious than money. Child named to extol parenthood in the face of financial inadequacy
457.	Ọnaamúti	The person whom they could not catch. Child born during or shortly after a "cat and mouse" conflict to prevent the child's birth, and the assailants failed
458.	Ònàọlápọ̀	The ways of honour are many. Child born when honour in different ways was being bestowed on the family members
459.	Ònàọpẹ́míípọ̀	The ways of my gratitude (to God) are many. Child born safely during a lot of family problems.
460.	Onítìjú	The one who is shy. Name given to a child who was born face down in areas of Yorùbáland when the common Àjàyí is not given to such child.
461.	Oore (Olúwa)	Kindness (of God)
462.	Ọrẹolúwa	The gift of God. Name given to a child by modern religionists
463.	Ọpẹ́àgbè	Thanks to Àgbè one of the family totems in old Ọ̀yọ́ Empire, or the super-fertile district so named in Àkókó
464.	Ọpẹ́míípọ̀	My thanks is much. Child born safely despite many complications or unforeseen negative occurrences
465.	Ọpẹ́odù	Thanks to Ifá corpus
466.	Ọpẹolú	Thanks to Olú, nowadays refers to Olúwa, God
467.	Ọpẹ́otù	Thanks to family totem Otù. Child born safely into an Otù family despite many unforeseen problems

	Name	Meaning and Circumstances
468.	Ọpẹ́ṣadé	Thanks made a crown. Child whose birth was made easy by being grateful to a previous benefactor
469.	Ọ̀rànlọ́lá	Rebellion or crime has honour. Child born when the father benefitted from a rebellion or social unrest
470.	Ọ̀rọ̀ótán	The word is not finished. Child born during a lingering family feud like disputed paternity of the child
471.	Ọṣọ́láké	Elite/Ornament at Aké (an area in Abẹ́okúta). Child born to an Ẹ̀gbá family resident far away from home (Aké)
472.	Ọ̀tọ̀lórìn	He walked separately. Child born under unique unusual circumstances during birth in the labour room
473.	Ọwádayọ̀	The paramount (Ìjẹ̀ṣà) chief's title has become joy. Child born to a non-Ìjẹ̀ṣà man married to an Ìjẹ̀ṣà woman
474.	Ọwọ̀adé	A column of crowns. Second or third child in a multiple birth incident to an Adé family
475.	Ọwọ̀ọ́ṣẹ́kù	Respect still remains, not finished
476.	(Ò)Pópọ́ọlá	The highway of honour. First son born after one or more daughters
477.	Suulọlá	Honour is limitless. Child born as an addition to many other children
478.	Ṣàṣàènià	Only very few people (recognize us when we are poor, it is the reverse when rich)
479.	Ṣíjúwọla	Open eyes to look at honour. A child that rarely opens his/her eyes during the first week of birth into an Ọlá family
480.	Ṣọlágbadé	Receive crown with honour. First child in an Adé family

	Name	Meaning and Circumstances
481.	Ṣubúloyè	Fall down into chieftaincy title. A premature child born to a new chief
482.	Ṣubulọlá	Fall down into honour. A premature child born into an Ọlá family
483.	Tanímọ̀lá	Who knows tomorrow? Child born at a time of significant social uncertainties or personal family uncertainties, that may include the death of the mother during the first week of the child's life, and expressed fears of the child's survival
484.	Tèmitọ́pẹ́	My own is good enough to be grateful for. Child born at a time the family just escaped or survived a calamity
485.	(Ọ̀)Tẹ̀mókùn	The rebellion has taken away okùn (the beaded wrist-band). Child born when a prominent member of an okùn family has just died in war or civil strife
486.	Tifálàṣẹ	Authority belongs to Ifá, the diviner
487.	Tínúoyè (wa)	From the inside of chieftaincy title (come). Child born by an Oyè mother to a father whose name of deity/totem as subject of the sentence has been cut off in usage
488.	Tinúọlá(de)	From the inside of honour (come). Child born by a mother from an Ọlá family into a family of deity/totem subject-name that has been cut off
489.	Títílayọ̀	Joy is forever. Child born at a time joyous occurrences continue to happen in the family
490.	Títílọlá	Honour is forever. Child born at a time occurrences of honour continue to occur in an Ọlá family
491.	Tiwalọlá	Honour belongs to us
492.	Tolúlọpẹ́	Thanks belongs to the king (Olú). Nowadays, it refers to God when a child arrives safely after some complications

	Name	Meaning and Circumstances
493.	Tolúfáṣẹ	What the Ifá diviner predicted has come to pass
494.	Tolúwalékè	God's action/decision proves supreme
495.	Tolúwanimí	I belong to God. Child whose mother died in the first week of birth
496.	Tọmọlawí	It is about the child that we talk. Parenthood is supreme at all cost
497.	Tọmọlójù	It is the child's that is paramount. Being a parent supersedes everything else. Child born at great expense
498.	(E)Wétúgà	The herb is up to a palace in social significance. Child born to a herbalist family and named to glorify the efficacy of herbs
499.	Wúràọlá	The gold of honour. Female first child born into an Ọlá family

Pet names, Nicknames and Titles that have become Surnames (Àwọn orúkọ Àlàbọrùn-tó-Dẹ̀wù)

	Name	Meaning
1.	Àbàtì	The untouchable/unconquerable wall (an abandoned house)
2.	Àbe	Populist person who is generous to outsiders but strongly miserly to members of his family, or a short thin hyperactive and rich person
3.	Àberìgìdí	Short, robust, hyperactive and rich man
4.	Abẹ́rẹ́òjé	Lead-needle. A very thin but effective person
5.	Abírí	We have given birth before (stop bluffing)
6.	Abólógún (Abólówógún)	He who settles down with the rich
7.	Abólórẹ́ (Abólówórẹ́)	He who befriends the rich
8.	Aburúmákùú	He who is too incorrigible to die
9.	Adágòjọ	He/She who walks with dainty steps
10.	Adágún	Lake, pool of water, a self-confident lone operator
11.	Adálémọ	He who builds a house specially for herbal preparations
12.	Adámọlúgbè	He who saves a child from punishment
13.	Adánláwọ̀	The one with the glistering –clear skin
14.	Adáralẹ́gbẹ́	The one who always looks good among his peers
15.	Adáralóùn	The one with the beautiful voice
16.	Adáramájà	He who is too handsome to be involved in a fight
17.	Adáramóyè	He who is well-fitted with a chieftaincy title
18.	Adáramọ́lá	He who is handsome in addition to having honour

	Name	Meaning
19.	Adàrán (borí iyàwó)	One who covers the bride's head with velvet cloth
20.	Adáraníjó	He who is beautiful to look at dancing
21.	Adáraníjọ	He who si good to have in one's group of comrades or congregation
22.	Adáranílà	He/She whose face is beautiful with tribal marks
23.	Adáraníwọ̀n	One endowed with just enough handsomeness (that would not attract the attention of witches)
24.	Adáunṣe	The independent farmer or herbalist
25.	Adégbẹ́ṣọ̀tẹ̀	He who creates a group specifically for rebellion
26.	Adẹ́gbẹ́yẹni	He whose presence among comrades is dignifying
27.	Adérùpọkọ̀	He who overloads the boat
28.	Adìgbòlùjà	He who collides with a fight, he who aggressively enters a battle, or fight
29.	Adínimọ́dò	He who blocks people off at the river with no room for escape
30.	Adùláwọ̀	The one with the black skin
31.	Adúmáàtí	The one whose black skin never fades, or never becomes ugly
32.	Adúrójà	The one who waits to fight or never runs from battle
33.	Afáríogun	He who clean-shaves the head of war. The warrior who brings home a lot of spoil from battle
34.	Afẹ́	Pet-name for a fun-loving, stylish-dressing teenage
35.	Afẹ́lamọ (bi ọyẹ́)	He who breezes people cold like the harmattan wind.
36.	Afẹ́rẹ̀	The light one, the portable one; short, thin person
37.	Afilaka	The very tall swinging one, who never snaps/breaks

	Name	Meaning
38.	Afowówẹ̀	One who is so rich that he bathes with money
39.	Àfọnjá	The African breadfruit fell off its tree (unto the head of the rebellious subject of the Aláàfin). An Aláàfin family cognomen
40.	Agírí	The strong, the tough, especially in battle
41.	Àgòrò	Supplies and logistics chieftain in the army
42.	Agúnbíadé	One who is straight as a crown on the king's head
43.	Agúnlóyè	Befittingly upright-seated on the throne
44.	Agbábíàká	One who is as agile as Àká, the shortened form of the title Ọnà-àká, the second of the three king-makers in the selection of an Aláàfin
45.	Agbájé	He who takes investments or money along unto his chieftaincy seat
46.	Àgbàọ̀jẹ̀	The elder worshipper in the ancestor – worship called Egúngún, the masquerade
47.	Àgbàsàlẹ̀	The elder downtown, or the ultimate arbiter of conflicts
48.	Àgbàtóògùn	The elder who is not tall (should not be annoyed, it is money that makes one walk tall)
49.	Àgbétì	One who can never be lifted off the ground, either because of his weight or his wrestling skills
50.	Àgbẹdẹ	The blacksmith's workshop. Pet-name for the blacksmith himself
51.	Agbẹ̀san-wàá	The one who avenges wrong-doing sharply and fearlessly
52.	Agbógùnún	The one who carries the deity of iron with dignity, and gives dignity to the deity
53.	Agbòjò	The one who receives or controls rain
54.	Agbọ́mábini	The one who hears that people gossip, or speak ill of him, and never queries them
55.	Agbọ́mábiwọ́n	Same as Agbọ́mábini
56.	Aìíkí	One who out of fear is never greeted by anybody who sees him

	Name	Meaning
57.	Àjàdí	Pet-name: people scramble to block him into the house so that they can have him exclusively
58.	Àjàdó	Male pet-name: people scramble to install him or settle him down
59.	Àjàkáyé	The one who fought all over the "world"
60.	Àjàlá	A pet-name: people scramble to (lick his body) be around him
61.	Àjànà	A chieftaincy title among the Òsùgbós
62.	Àjànàkú	The pet-name of the elephant adopted by human beings to signify large size and power
63.	Àjàní	The pet-name of a person so loved that people scramble to have him
64.	Ajánlékokò	Dog on a suicidal mission of chasing the wolf. Pet-name of someone who considers himself as the wolf; while his opponent is the dog
65.	Àjàó	Pet-name: people scramble to have a look at him
66.	Ajáṣin	A princely title or high chief title
67.	Ajé	Investment or Money
68.	Ajénifújà	Money is what makes it possible to throw party and invite a live band to play, in order to brag
69.	Ajépé	Financial Investments are profitable or wise
70.	Ajẹpẹ́(ayé)	Long-lasting enjoyment (of life)
71.	Ajíboṣo	One who wakes up to worship the "wise" god Orìṣà-oko
72.	Ajídàgbà	One who wakes up to grow older every day (like the banana tree)
73.	Àjídáùn	One who is aroused from sleep and vocally answers
74.	Àjídáun	One who is aroused from sleep and makes compensatory demands for waking him up
75.	Ajíga (bí ọgẹ̀dẹ̀)	Daily (fast) growing child (like the banana tree)

	Name	Meaning
76.	Ajígbólámu	One who drinks honour at waking up in the morning
77.	Ajijẹdídùn	He who wakes up to eat what is sweet
78.	Àjikẹ́	She who is aroused from sleep in order to be pampered
79.	Ajíkòbí	He who wakes up to meet the whole family daily; a uniquely loved child
80.	Àjílà	An aláàfin totem – one who makes his wake-up caller wealthy
81.	Ajilóre	One who wakes up to have relatives, or one who has relatives very early in life
82.	Ajímọ́kọ́	A successful farmer – one who picks up the hoe on waking up
83.	Ajírire	One who wakes up to experience good things
84.	Ajírọtútù	He who forges cold iron very early in the morning at the blacksmith workshop
85.	Ajiṣafẹ́	One who wakes up to socialize stylishly
86.	Ajiṣebútú	Strong farmer who wakes up to raise dust daily
87.	Ajiṣefínní	One who wakes up to behave daintily with perfection
88.	Ajíṣegírí	One who wakes up to behave smartly
89.	Ajíṣekọ́lá	One who wakes up to collect or assemble honour
90.	Ajíṣọmọ	One who wakes up to behave like a spoilt child
91.	Àjọbọ	One who must be collectively worshipped like a god
92.	Ajọ́lọ́wẹ̀	One who accepts invitation to communal labour in one other person's farm, communally-spirited man
93.	Àjọmọ	A chieftaincy title
94.	Ajòmàle	One who looks like (resembles) a Muslim
95.	Ajósẹ̀	The worshipper (of a named deity) on its sacred day
96.	Àjùwọ̀n	Name of an Ọ̀yọ́ family totem or chieftaincy title

	Name	Meaning
97.	Akánimọ́dò	One who meets us at the river against our wish
98.	Àkànle	A male pet-name: something nailed down hard
99.	Akápò	The treasurer
100.	Akérédolú-ale	The small-in-stature that became the most prominent (son) of Ale (a person)
101.	Akéréle	Small and hard (tough)
102.	Akésọ́dẹ̀	The one who calls loudly at the hunter (loud and ringing voice)
103.	Akéùlà	The one who studies the Arabic language and becomes wealthy
104.	Akéúṣọlá	The one who studies the Arabic language as a thing of honour
105.	Àkẹ́jù	The over pampered
106.	Àko	The chieftaincy title of the king's super messenger
107.	Akogun	A military rule
108.	Akọṣílè	The clerk who writes cash (shilling, colonial coin)
109.	Akúrú(mágọ̀)	The short man (who is not stupid)
110.	Aládésurú	The crowned one who fellowships with similar people, or who gives birth to "chips off the old block"
111.	Aladéesúùrù	The crown-prince of patience
112.	Alága	The Chairman (traditionally, the judge who sits in the chair)
113.	Alágbàáà	An ancestor-worshippers' chieftaincy
114.	Alákàá	The owner of the barn
115.	Alákijà	The title of the king of Ìkijà
116.	Alámùútú	The successful herbalist who prides himself in releasing medicinally/psychically bound or afflicted people
117.	Aláràn-án	The owner of velvet cloth

	Name	Meaning
118.	Alárápe	He who has relatives in complete attendance
119.	Alásà	The owner of the shield, an Òṣògbò chieftaincy
120.	Alébíoṣù	The one who appears spectacularly like a new moon
121.	Alebíowú	He who is as hard as the blacksmith's iron mallet
122.	Alégẹ	The one who appears/poses spectacularly in a sitting posture
123.	Alejúleùn	One who hardens his face and speaks with a harsh voice
124.	Alèmẹrù	One who is capable of capturing/dispelling fear
125.	Alẹ́gbẹ́	One who has age-group or comrades
126.	Alẹ́gbẹ́lẹ́yẹ	One who has comrades has dignity
127.	Àlòkò	See Àlùkò
128.	Alókoláṛọ	A farmer and blacksmith or one who possesses a farm and possesses many cutlasses/blacksmith workshop
129.	Alóngẹ́	The thing tall one, the under-weight one
130.	Alówónle	He who has money at home
131.	Alọ́(máàjá)	Thin; the one who twists (without snapping)
132.	Alọ́ba(lọ́rẹ́ẹ́)	The one who has the king as a friend
133.	Àlùkò	The name of a rare purple-feathered bird
134.	Amélè	The one who takes the cutlass, a hard working farmer
135.	Amòye	The wise, the one who has intelligence
136.	Àmọ̀yè	Know him and be cured of your illness
137.	Àmùrè(oògùn)	Girdle/War dress (of medicine/psychic power)
138.	Àńjọọ́rìn	We all work together as comrades (without knowing who among us will be rich)

	Name	Meaning
139.	Aníbaba	The owner of father. One who declares that he has a father to be proud of, and therefore not be afraid
140.	Anífálájé	The wealthy diviner; one who has the Ifá oracle and also has wealth
141.	Anífowóṣe	He who has something to do with money, he has something to spend money on
142.	Anígilájé	The prosperous timber merchant
143.	Aníkiláyà	The brave; one who has courage in his chest (like thunder); the pet-name of a popular Ìjẹ̀bú king
144.	Aníkúlapó	One who has death in the quiver. One who always has arrows in his quiver; ever-ready warrior
145.	Anímáṣaun	The generous; one who gives out freely of his possessions
146.	Aníṣulówó	He who has yams and also has money – the rich yam farmer
147.	Apálowó	The arm is money – it is work that one does with one's arm that will bring money
148.	Apámpá	The capable; the arm is behaving like the arm should. A chieftaincy title of the elders' emissary
149.	Apániṣílẹ̀	The arm is shilling (money). It is the work one does with one's arm that brings money
150.	Àpáta	The rock. A pet-name
151.	Apèènà	The title of a high chief among the Òsùgbós or Ògbónis elders' council that used to be powerful enough to control the king
152.	Apélógun	One who is complete in battle/war. The brave who is most efficient when in active battle
153.	Àràbà	The title of the president of the herbalists'/ diviners' council, or association
154.	Àrẹ	The supreme leader, most prominent of which is the military leader's title - Àrẹ Ọ̀nàkakaǹfò
155.	Arẹ́gbẹ́	Shortened form of Arẹ́gbẹ́ṣọlá

	Name	Meaning
156.	Arẹ́gbẹ́ṣọlá	One who behaves with dignity when he sees his comrades or one who always has a group of comrades to bluff with
157.	Arẹ́gbẹ́yẹni	One who always has a group of comrades to dignify behaviours
158.	Àrẹ̀mọ	The heir apparent
159.	Àrẹ̀mú	A male pet-name. Begged to be (caught) born
160.	Àrẹoyè	The (leader) most important/senior chieftaincy title
161.	Àrẹ̀sà	The title of the paramount chief/king of Ìresà
162.	Aríbáṣoyè	One who is always around to celebrate chieftaincy with
163.	Aribátiṣé	One who always finds a way to solve problems
164.	Aríbidésí	One who always finds a place to stay as a guest
165.	Aríibìyọ̀	One who is joyous at sighting relatives
166.	Arígbábù(owó)	One who always finds a (calabash) large container to scoop money (coins)
167.	Aríjájẹ	One who always finds something to eat (ever buoyant)
168.	Aríṣekọ́lá	One who finds things to do to assemble honour
169.	Àró	An Ògbóni title
170.	Aróbíẹkẹ́	One who is as upright as the standing house-support; forked pole
171.	Arógẹ	One who stands daintily in a dignified manner
172.	Arógundádé	One who puts a crown on when he sees an opposing army. A man glad to go to war. A fearless warrior
173.	Arógunrẹ́ẹ̀rín	The professional warrior who laughs (is happy) when a war breaks out
174.	Arójò	Shortened form of Arójòjoyè

	Name	Meaning
175.	Arójòjoyè	He has enough rain when becoming a king. One of the cognomens of an ancient Ìjẹ̀bú king during whose coronation there was a heavy downpour of rain
176.	Arómáṣọdú	The indigo dye is the thing that darkens the (otherwise bright) cloth
177.	Arómáyẹ̀	Steadfast support
178.	Arómọláàrán	One who clothes (his) children in velvet
179.	Aróñkọ́lá	A contracted form of Aróúnkọ́là
180.	Aróúnkọ́là	One who finds something to collect honour with
181.	Arówóbùsóyè	One who finds money to put into chieftaincy
182.	Arówójolú	One who finds money to be made the paramount chief or king
183.	Arówójọ̀bẹ̀	One who finds money to cook and eat palatable stew
184.	Arówólò	One who always finds money to (use) spend
185.	Arówóṣafẹ̀	One who has enough money for a stylish and comfortable (leisurely) living
186.	Arówóṣayé	One who has money to live comfortably
187.	Arówóṣere	One who always has money to play or throw parties with
188.	Arówóṣọlá	One who has money to bluff with or behave honourably with
189.	Arọ́bajẹ	One who always finds a kingship to be enthroned to
190.	Arọ̀jò(ọlà)	One who rains (wealth) on other people
191.	Arọ̀lóyè	One who is easy on the crown – a king whose reign is very prosperous for the people
192.	Arúléba	One who finds a house to (hide) live in
193.	Arúwàjoyè	One whose (good) character made him worthy to be a chief/king
194.	Àsálù	The protector to run to. An Ògbóni chieftaincy title

	Name	Meaning
195.	Asánńdè	One who wears medicinal leather bands around his waist
196.	Asándẹ	A chieftaincy title. One who wears a brass waist-band
197.	Àṣágìdìgbì	A pet-name for a very agile, though heavily built short man – the solid hawk
198.	Àṣayè / Àṣáyè	One who is born to survive
199.	Aṣebẹbẹ	The wonderful performer or achiever
200.	Àṣekún	Additional investments (do not allow wealth/money) to finish
201.	Aṣímọlọ́wọ́(ọ̀tẹ̀)	He who always uses greater force to stop a recalcitrant person from being rebellious
202.	Aṣọ̀gbọ́n	An Ògbóni chieftaincy title
203.	Aṣúbíaró	One who is (dresses) dark blue like indigo dye
204.	Aṣúbiòjò	One who is dark-dressed like the rain cloud
205.	Atẹkojà	The successful spy who steps (quietly) on the farm to fight in war
206.	Àtéwọ́lará	The palm constitutes relatives. One can only be sure of (family) support from one's hand used to work for money
207.	Atófaratì	One, strong enough to lean on (like a mountain)
208.	Atótilétọ̀	One who is important enough for one to specially visit from one's house
209.	Atóbatẹ́lẹ̀	Naturally well-built like a king, therefore needs no chieftaincy
210.	Atúnramú	One who equips and re-equips himself (is not let down, or does not lose face often)
211.	Atúnraṣe	One who grooms himself properly
212.	Awẹ́	A chip off the old block of a renowned ancestor
213.	Awẹ́lẹ́	Shortened form of Awẹ́lẹ́ńjẹ́. A delicately framed but powerful man
214.	Awẹ́lẹ́ńjẹ́	A delicately framed but powerful man
215.	Awẹ́lẹ́(wà)	Pet-name for female of cool, detailed, beautiful slenderness

Name	Meaning
216. Awọ́nbíọgbọ́n	Scarce wisdom
217. Ayéfẹ́lẹ́	Life is delicately thin (fragile)
218. Ayélabọ́lá	Honour is met in the world. It is not brought in at birth
219. Ayélọtítí	World without end
220. Àyìnká	Praised all over. A male pet-name
221. Badà	One of the junior military titles
222. Bájùláyé	Father is most important in life. A chieftaincy title
223. Balógun	Military commander
224. Baṣọ̀run	The Prime Minister, and diviner of the king's (heaven) head
225. Báṣùà	An ògbóni chieftaincy title
226. Bíbílọlá	Good ancestry connotes honour
227. Bólódeòkú	If the owner of the garden/premises does not die (the premises will not be overgrown with weeds)
228. Bòṁbàtà	Use a shoe to slap (him/her) many times
229. Bọ̀rọ̀kìnní	Financially secure gentleman who also looks well-fed
230. Dálémọ	See Adálémọ
231. Dálùúmọ̀	Know the town on your own
232. Dáǹmọlé	Own Islam alone as a private property
233. Dáódù	The first son and heir to the father's title(s)
234. Dáramọ́lá	Handsome in addition to having honour
235. Dárópalé	Prepare indigo suspension specifically to dye the floor of the house, beautifully
236. Díẹ̀kọ́lọlá	Well-bred; honour is much on me
237. Èdìdì (tí a mú dìrókò, ara ló fi san)	The smothering bind (put round the iroko tree made the tree get fatter, instead of getting thinner)

	Name	Meaning
238.	Èjí	The natural or artificial tooth-gap in upper or lower incisors
239.	Èjígbádéró	Èjí holds down the crown in place
240.	Èkémọdé	The young jester
241.	Elébùútè	The owner/keeper of the marine beach
242.	Èsúrúoṣó	An exceptionally light-skinned man from an Oṣó family (Òrìṣà-oko worshippers)
243.	Eyínfúnjowó	Teeth whiter than money (silver coins)
244.	Ẹgbẹ́yẹmí	Comradeship makes me dignified
245.	Ẹgbẹ́délé	My comrade (will) get home with me
246.	Ẹjalónibú	The deep waters belong to fish
247.	Ẹlẹ́kùú	The designer/keeper of masquerade masks
248.	Ẹlẹ́mọ	A chieftaincy title
249.	Ẹlẹ́mọrọ̀	The Ẹlẹ́mọ of wealth, a very rich person
250.	Ẹlẹ́ṣọ́ọ́	The elegant, highly decked with ornaments
251.	Ẹ̀míàbàtà	The potency of the marsh/swampy land
252.	Ẹ̀ṣọ́	Ornaments/Fashion
253.	Fàdákà	Silver
254.	Fínní	Super-clean; detailed
255.	Gíwá	A chieftaincy title
256.	Gólóbà	A very tall and stooped person
257.	Gbajúmọ̀	Well-known/popular elite (200 eyes know him/her)
258.	(A)Gbálájọbí	The whole community collectively gives birth to it
259.	(A)Gbẹ́bọlájà	Puts the sacrifice on the house-ceiling (for rituals)
260.	(A)Gbólóge (níyì)	One who makes the fashionable to be respected – the goldsmith

	Name	Meaning
261.	Ìdíàgbọn	By the coconut tree (father whose house is)
262.	Ìdíàgbọn (kò şeé şebùsò)	One cannot make the foot of the coconut tree a resting place (the fruit might drop anytime)
263.	Igińlá	A rare exceptionally durable and large tree (*Okwubaca aubriville*), believed to have psychic powers
264.	Ìpàyẹ́	The name given to the plundering soldiers of Ògèdèǹgbé of Iléşà
265.	Ìşọ́lá	A pet-name
266.	Jàfójo	Fight for the coward or weak person
267.	Jágilégbò (soògùn)	Yank off the tree's root (for medicine)
268.	Jagun	A military title
269.	(A)Jàmgbàdì	A rabble-rouser
270.	Jáwáńdò	The aggressive and robust one comes to the river
271.	Jéjé	A popular young man who behaves easy-come easy-go with his money
272.	Jẹ́gẹ́dẹ́	A gangling tender person
273.	Jẹ́jẹ́	Easy, very easy, peaceful behavior
274.	Jèbútú	He who plays aggressively and confidently (to raise dust)
275.	Jògbòdó	An ebullient, usually overweight teenager
276.	(Adì)Káká	Over-dressed, over-armoured for purpose
277.	Kánípé	Let-us-say-that (a colloquial mannerism)
278.	(I)Kánmọdi	Termites build a wall (without the fear of the rain)
279.	Kẹkẹ	The rattling mouth
280.	Kẹ́kẹ́	The highly beautifying Òwu facial marks
281.	(A)Kẹ́lẹ́kọ̀ọ́	One who teaches the teacher a resounding experience

Name	Meaning
282. Kobíowú	As hard sounding as the blacksmith's mallet
283. Kókóirin	The natural side lump of iron
284. (A)Kọ́mọláfẹ́	He who teaches a child (people) how to enjoy themselves
285. (A)Kọ̀wé	The town clerk
286. Lágùdà	A chieftaincy title
287. Lèmọ́mù	A Muslim title of he who leads the congregation in prayer
288. Líṣàbí	Selector of people for a special human breeding program
289. Mádàáríkàn	Do not confront
290. Májà	Do not fight/quarrel
291. Májàṣán	Do not eat any meal without meat
292. (Adán) Máṣàá	He who glitters without fading
293. (Adára) Máṣàá	He who is handsome without fading
294. Moṣọbalájé	I am king among investors
295. Mọ́gàjí	A heir apparent (Hausa origin)
296. Òbe	A small-statured, but agile person
297. Òbébé (yeúyeú)	A portable, neat, handsome and smart man
298. Òdógiyún	Super fertile stud (he who impregnates wood)
299. Ògèdèǹgbé	Standing upright (to fight)
300. Ògégbò	He who cuts a tree-root (a renowned herbalist)
301. Ògìdán	The tall heavily-muscled lone ranger (pet-name of the tiger)
302. Ògúnòde	The public iron-deity (to be feared)
303. Òjíjí	The shocker, the super stimulant/catalyst
304. Òjíkùtù	He who wakes up early, habitually
305. Ojúkòtì	Not ashamed (vulture, not to eat roadside sacrifice)

	Name	Meaning
306.	Òkèńlá	Big mountain (that cannot be easily climbed)
307.	Òkí	An ancient cognomen for Adéyẹmi (Aláàfin)
308.	Òkúpẹ̀	The "dressed" corpse is standing straight without leaning in any direction
309.	Okùúpẹ̀	The beaded wrist-band chieftaincy is not about to be lost by the family
310.	Òkòorò	The stone (missile) of Orò, the curfew deity
311.	Olísà	A political chieftaincy title
312.	Olórunlékòó	The renowned warrior in Lagos
313.	Olókè	The owner of the mountain. The person who leads during the worship of the mountain
314.	Olókùnọlà	He who has the rope of wealth; the harbinger of wealth
315.	Olorì	The king's wife
316.	Olóṣi	An Ògbóni chieftaincy title (in charge of Edọn)
317.	Olókodáná	The farmer who makes fire for his meal on the farm
318.	Olótùú	The leader (nowadays the compere of radio and television programmes)
319.	Olówófẹlá	The rich extends honour
320.	Olówóòfóyèkù	The rich cannot but have chieftaincy titles
321.	Olówógúnlẹ̀	The rich possesses land at will
322.	Olówójẹ̀bútú	The rich plays around aggressively to raise dust, or to be recognized
323.	Olówójolú	The rich is more prominent than the king (olú)
324.	Olówókóre	The rich collects good luck
325.	Olówókúre	The dialect variant of Olówókóre
326.	Olowóòkéré	The small-statured rich cannot be termed small
327.	Olówólèkómọ̀	It is only the rich that Èkó (Lagos) recognises

#	Name	Meaning
328.	Olówómẹyẹ	The rich knows what is dignifying
329.	Olówóníílárá	It is only the rich who has many relations
330.	Olówópọ̀rọ̀kú (rẹnfẹ́nrẹnfẹ́n)	The rich solves all problems with money; kills all court-cases or conflicts (completely)
331.	Olówóyẹyè	The rich is fit for a chieftaincy title, or makes chieftaincy dignifying
332.	Olówóyọ (bi ọjọ́)	The rich appears in glory (like the morning sun)
333.	Olówu	The title of the king of Òwu town
334.	Ọlọ́ọrunnínbẹ	It is only God who is
335.	Olúñlọ́yọ̀ọ́	He is a king (Olú) in Ọ̀yọ́ town
336.	Olúṣí	A chieftaincy title
337.	Olùwá	A chieftaincy title
338.	Onígbàǹjo	The auctioneer
339.	Olúwo	An Ògbóni / Òṣùgbó chieftaincy title
340.	Oníbìíyọ̀	He who has pedigree rejoices
341.	Onibọnòjé	The one with the lead-ringed gun-barrel
342.	Oníbùdó	The undisputed owner of the settlement (a pet-name for the lion)
343.	Onibùjé	The professional tattooist with the bùjé fruit-juice
344.	Onígbòde	The dominant person in town
345.	Oníkerú	A chieftaincy title
346.	Oníkòsì	The title of the king of Ìkòsì town
347.	Oníkòyí	The title of the king of Ìkòyí town, the historical town of super-archers and warriors
348.	Onílé - eré	A chieftaincy title
349.	Onilẹ̀	The landlord
350.	Onímọlẹ̀	The owner (lead worshipper) of earth-spirits, of named deities

	Name	Meaning
351.	Onírù	A chieftaincy title
352.	Onítìrẹ́	The title of the king of Itìrẹ́
353.	Onítọ̀lọ̀	The title of the king of Ìtọ̀lọ́
354.	Oníyangí	The rabble-rouser (owner of laterite rocks)
355.	Onígà	The owner of the palace
356.	Oníyẹlú	A chieftaincy title (the one who is fit for the town)
357.	Oríràrán	The one who is destined to be rich to buy velvet
358.	Òríràrán	The one who makes people rich at first contact to buy velvet
359.	Osárénówó	One who makes money fast, gets rich quick
360.	Òṣòdi	A chieftaincy title (the inner-room counselor)
361.	Owóẹ̀yẹ	The money/wealth of dignity
362.	Owókòníran	Money has no ancestry, wealth is not an ascribed attribute; anyone can be rich
363.	Owólawí	It is money we are talking of
364.	Owólẹbí	Money creates family relations
365.	Owólayé	Money is life
366.	Owólòwò	Money is imperative for commerce
367.	Owòrú	A chieftaincy title
368.	Ọbalọ́la	Heir apparent (future king)
369.	Ọbaníkòró	A chieftaincy title. The original Ọbaníkòró was reported to be fearless and tactless
370.	Ọdẹòperin	The (local) hunter never kills an elephant; an advice that one should know one's limits
371.	Òdọ̀fin	A chieftaincy title
372.	Ògínní	An Ìjẹ̀ṣà chieftaincy title
373.	Òjọrá	An (Àwórì) chieftaincy title
374.	Òjọmu	An Oǹdó chieftaincy title

Name	Meaning
375. Ọkanlọmọ	Child is child, male or female
376. Ọkùnrinmẹ́ẹ̀ta	An exceptionally brave man (three men)
377. Ọlẹ́ṣin	A chieftaincy title, probably the calvary chief
378. Ọlọ́gbẹ́ńlá	The one who inflicts wide and deep wounds on the enemy in battle
379. Ọlọ́kọ̀	The one who carves boats, or who paddles boats
380. Ọlọ́nííyọ̀	The person who has relatives is joyous
381. Ọlọ́runnímbẹ	It is God that "is"
382. Ọlọ́tọ̀	The chieftaincy title of the head of Ọ̀tọ̀ community/town
383. Ọmọ́lúàbí	A properly cultured or well-behaved person
384. Ọmọọba	The prince or princess
385. Ọràngún	The title of Ìlá king
386. Ọ́rẹ̀àgbà	The (humble) friend of elders
387. Ọlọ́jọ	A chieftaincy title
388. Ọlọ́jọ́	The celebrant. A festival in Ìlé-Ìfẹ
389. Ọ̀rọ̀mpọ̀tọ́	The name of one of the kings of Ọ̀yọ́ empire, now denotes the "fat one"
390. Ọ̀rọ̀npọ̀tọ́	Same as Ọ̀rọ̀mpọ̀tọ́
391. Pàràkòyí	A chieftaincy title in Ìbàdàn
392. Sàrákí	A very wealthy and popular chief (Hausa origin)
393. Sarùmí	The military title of the commander of calvary
394. Séríkí	Commander of young warriors, mostly rookies in battle encounters
395. Sàṣẹrẹ́	A chieftaincy title in Ońdó town
396. Ṣàpárà	The joker, humorist
397. Ṣapará	A medium-sized agbádá dress or a chieftaincy title

	Name	Meaning
398.	Ṣígunmárù	He who is never tired of waging wars
399.	Ṣọ́nibárẹ́	Watch out as to who you befriend
400.	(A)Tàkùrọ́ (tàpòtàpò)	The palm-kernel merchant (who sells with the bags)
401.	Tañtọ́lọ́run	Who is as powerful as God?
402.	Tèmiyémi	My behavior is understandable/rational to me
403.	Tewétegbò (loògùn)	Both leaves and roots are medicine
404.	(Ẹ̀dá) Tómọ̀la (ò sí)	No one knows tomorrow
405.	Yagbóyajù	All conquering destroyer of forests and jungles

Common Traditional Pet-Names Or Affectionate Names (Female)

	Name	Meaning
1.	Àbẹ̀bí	Begged to be born
2.	Àbẹ̀gbé	Begged to be carried/had
3.	Àbẹ̀kẹ́	Begged to be pampered
4.	Àbẹ̀mú	Begged to be taken/possessed
5.	Àbẹ̀ní	Begged to be had/possessed
6.	Àbẹ̀ó	Begged to be looked at
7.	Àdùfẹ́	One whom people scramble to love
8.	Àdùkẹ́	One whom people scramble to pamper
9.	Àdùnní	Sweet to have/possess
10.	Àdùnọlá	The sweetness of honour
11.	Àgbékẹ́	Carried around to pamper
12.	Àjíkẹ́	One who is woken up to be pampered
13.	Àjíún	One who bluffs at being woken up
14.	Àkànkẹ́	One whom to meet is to pamper, or one who is always pampered on contact
15.	Àlàkẹ́	One who is selectively pampered in detail
16.	Àmọ̀kẹ́	One who is pampered, once she is known
17.	Àníkẹ́	One who is possessed to be pampered
18.	Àpékẹ́	All people must assemble to jointly pamper her
19.	Àpèkẹ́	One who is called/invited to be pampered
20.	Àpínkẹ́	One who is pampered in turns
21.	Àríkẹ́	One who is pampered at sight

22.	Àrán-àntí	The velvet never loses its fame/popularity
23.	Àrán-òntí	Same as Àrán-àntí
24.	Àsùnkẹ́	One whom we (sleep) lie down to pamper
25.	Àṣàní	Selected to be born, or product of selective breeding
26.	Àṣàkẹ́	Selected to be pampered or product of selective breeding
27.	Àṣàkún	Selected fully, or to be added to others
28.	Àṣàníkẹ́ẹ́	Specially selected to possess for pampering
29.	Àtọ́kẹ́	One who is given very selective pampering
30.	Awélọ́rùn (bi ikòtó)	The one with the beautifully ridged neck (like the shell of the periwinkle
31.	Awẹ́lẹ́wà	Cool or properly detailed in beauty
32.	Àwẹ̀ní	The one to watch and possess
33.	Àwẹ̀ró	Bathed or washed to wait for (pampering, dressing, feeding, etc.)
34.	Àyọ̀ká	One around whom people remain joyous
35.	Ayílukọ	The plump/rotund one who rolls into her husband in bed
36.	Àyìnkẹ́	Praise to be pampered
37.	Bẹ́wàjí	Wakes up with beauty
38.	Èjí	Tooth-gap incisors, upper or lower
39.	Èjídé	Tooth-gap has arrived
40.	(Ẹlẹ́yinjú) Ẹgẹ́	The one with delicate eye-balls
41.	Ibàdíàrán	The buttocks of velvet or for velvet clothing
42.	Ìdi -Ìlẹ̀kẹ̀	The waist for coral beads ornamentation
43.	Jíbẹ́wà	Wakes up and sees beauty around
44.	Kẹ̀kẹ̀	Enthusiastic behavior (towards her husband)
45.	(Adú) Máadán	Black beauty. The black that shines

46.	Òdèré	The dove, peaceful
47.	Olóókọ	Name-sake (same name with a senior wife, a female in-law, or an elderly female in the house)
48.	Òreñté	Portable, short and thin
49.	Oyinlọ́lá	Honour is honey
50.	Ọpẹ́lẹ́ngẹ́	Slim and beautiful woman
51.	Òwúrubutu	Plump round (like a tailor's thread of such shape)
52.	Sẹ̀gi	Blue tubular beads
53.	Sẹ̀gilọlá	Blue tubular beads constitute honour
54.	Sẹ̀gilọ́lá	As precious as blue tubular beads in honour

Common Traditional Pet-Names Or Affectionate Names (Male)

	Name	Meaning
1.	Àdèyí	He who turns round to release himself when bound
2.	Àdìó	He who is glanced at when packaged
3.	Àdìgún	He who is packed straight/upright
4.	Àdìsá	Package or tie him, and run away
5.	Àjàdí	He who fights to the last man, or fought for as the last precious thing
6.	Àjàdó	He who fights to establish a settlement, or fought for to establish/settle him
7.	Àjàgbé	He who fights to take, or fought for before being carried/possessed
8.	Àjàlá	He who fights to be wealthy, or the whirlwind makes him wealthy
9.	Àjàmú	He who fights to take or get, or fought for to be taken/possessed
10.	Àjàní	He who fights to possess, or fought for to be had/possessed
11.	Àjàpé	He who fights to excel, or fought for to be complete/excel
12.	Àjàó	He who fights to look at something he wants, or fought for to look at
13.	Ajíṣe	He with early morning activities
14.	Ajiṣefínní	He with early morning activity to be super-clean
15.	Àkànbí	He whose turn it is to arrive, or asked for to arrive
16.	Àkàndé	Same as Àkànbí
17.	Ajiṣegírí	He with early morning activity to be ever ready
18.	Àkàngbé	He whose turn it is to possess, or asked for to be carried/possessed
19.	Àkànjí	He whose turn it is to wake up, or called upon to wake up

	Name	Meaning
20.	Àkànmú	He whose turn it is to take, or asked for to be possessed
21.	Àkànní	He whose turn it is to possess, or one who was possessed according to schedule
22.	Àkàn-ó	He whose turn it is to gaze, or asked for to look at
23.	Alàbí	Immaculate white cloth give birth to, or split up to be born (originally given to multiple-birth children only)
24.	Àlàdé	One who is the first son after three or more daughters, or immaculate white cloth binds him as sacred
25.	Àlàmú	Immaculate white takes this
26.	Àlàó	Immaculate white looks at this
27.	Àlàwó	Same as Àlàó
28.	Àmàó	One who is looked at, once he is known
29.	Àmọdá	One who is known for cure
30.	Àmọlé	One who is superfluously known
31.	Àmọ́ó	One who is looked at, once he is known
32.	Àrèó	The one who is pampered to look at
33.	Apáta	The rock
34.	Arówólò	He who always finds money to use
35.	Àṣàmú	The one selectively taken
36.	Àtàndá	Flattened to be created
37.	Atítẹ̀ẹ́bí	One born on a prepared throne/cradle
38.	Àyìnká	Praised all over everywhere
39.	Àyìnlá	Praised or flattered to be "licked"
40.	Eyín-afẹ́	Any teeth we like (is what we chew with)
41.	Ẹniọlá	A person of honour
42.	Fínní	Super-clean, dainty

	Name	Meaning
43.	Ìṣọ̀lá	Honourable behavior
44.	Ìyàndá	Famine ends. First son after many daughters
45.	Iyìọlá	The prestige of honour
46.	(Adán) Máṣàá	He who glitters beautifully without fading
47.	(Adára) Máṣàá	He who is constantly handsome
48.	Olóókọ	Name-sake (of husband, or male family order)
49.	Olówó	The rich, the one who has money
50.	Òpóadé	The pillar of crown
51.	Òpóọlá	The pillar of honour
52.	(Agùn) Táṣọọ́lò	Tall enough to wear clothes prestigiously

Àbíkú (Born-To-Die-In-Infancy) Names

These are names given to children that were believed to be members of a group of spirit-nymphs, who take on mortal existence to be born, only to die and return to their group at times already specified by the group, before they were born.

Modern medicine states that sickle-cell disease and its complications along with malnutrition were responsible for the deaths. Hence, the àbíkú syndrome is not prominent nowadays.

	Name	Meaning
1.	Aájúwò	It will be possible to take care of this child
2.	Ààtàndá	The dunghill (where dead babies are buried) is lonely
3.	Ààtandáre	The dunghill proclaims good news that the child will not die
4.	Abíiná	We have given birth to it, but its survival is dicey
5.	Adékògbẹ́	He arrives to reject the bush (grave)
6.	Ágbèéjúlée	We do not have any hope in him
7.	Ajá	Dog. A highly insulting/degrading name that is believed will make him to be rejected by the group and therefore stay alive
8.	Ajéiígbé	Money must never be totally lost (spent on the child)
9.	Ajídàgbà	He who grows every morning (Child's survival is reckoned by the day)
10.	Àjídáùn	He who answers each time he is woken from sleep
11.	Ajitòní	He who wakes up today, although we are not sure whether he will wake up tomorrow
12.	Àkísààtán	We are short of rags (to wrap baby-corpse)

	Name	Meaning
13.	Akújí	He who dies and wakes
14.	Aláwààyè	This is a coming (being born) to survive
15.	Àléèlọ	He who is driven away (as a nymph) but refuses to go
16.	Àmbẹlọ́run	We are appealing to God
17.	Àmbẹlọ́un	Same as Àmbẹlọ́run
18.	Ámọnúrẹ̀	We do not know its mind
19.	Àndùú	We are struggling (for its survival)
20.	Aníkúté	One who dies (as a baby) loses respect
21.	Àńwòó	We are keeping an eye on it
22.	Àńwóókọ	We are searching for a name (see Orúkọtán)
23.	Àpáàrà	Thunder; child that comes and goes with devastating effect on the mother
24.	Arádojo	We have become cowards
25.	Arirí	We have seen it before
26.	Àṣádé	The hawk has come
27.	Àṣáyè	We give birth to it to survive
28.	Àṣìńwòó	We are still looking at it
29.	Àtińmọ́ọ́	We have been knowing it before
30.	Atóyèbí	We have given birth to chieftaincy again
31.	Atóyẹbí	It is time you befit, or give dignity to pedigree
32.	Ayédùn	Life is sweet (survive to enjoy it)
33.	Ayékùn-ún	The world is not full
34.	Ayélàágbé	It is only in the world that life is for us to live
35.	Ayémọ̀wá	People know us for notoriety (of infant mortality)

	Name	Meaning
36.	Ayọ́runbọ̀	He who has gone to heaven and returned
37.	Bádéjókòó	Sit (settle) with the crown
38.	Bámbẹ̀ẹ́	Beg him/her for me
39.	Bámidúró	Stay with me
40.	Bámiṣayé	Enjoy life with me
41.	Bámiṣilé	Open (establish) the house with me
42.	Bámmẹ́kẹ́	Help me take the roofing thatch/forked (house) corner post
43.	Báñjókòó	Sit (settle down) with me
44.	Báñkọ́lé	Build the house with me
45.	Báyéwú	Develop (grow big) with the world
46.	Béyìíòkú	If this does not die...
47.	Biòbákú	If he/she does not die...
48.	Bólúdúró	Stay (stand) with the king or depend on God only
49.	Bólújókòó	Stay (sit) with the king
50.	Bóokúotẹ́	You lose all respect, if you die
51.	Bọ́lájókòó	Sit (settle down) with honour
52.	Búlùúró	Stay with the town
53.	Dáìíní	Holds on to this
54.	Dáìró	Prevents this from dying
55.	Dáìísí	Keeps this alive
56.	Dẹ̀indé	Comes back
57.	Dẹ̀yìnbọ̀	Comes back
58.	(Ará) Dojo	We have become cowards
59.	Dúródọlá	Stay to have and enjoy honour

	Name	Meaning
60.	Dúrójayé	Stay to enjoy life
61.	Dúróoríkẹ́ẹ́	Stay to experience pampering
62.	Dúróṣarọ	Stay to operate the blacksmith shop
63.	Dúrósinmí	Stay to survive me (to bury me)
64.	Dúrótoyè	Stay and enjoy the chieftaincy
65.	Dúrówojú	Stay to look at faces (of the world)
66.	Égbáyélọ	It continues to live in the world
67.	Èkétundé	The treacherous has come again
68.	Epódùn	Palm oil is sweet (survive to enjoy it)
69.	Epóyùn	Palm oil is sweet (survive to enjoy it) - Ìjẹ̀bú
70.	Ẹniayékàn	Living in the world is now its turn
71.	Ẹniayéwù	One who likes the world (and will survive)
72.	Ẹniìgbọ̀kàn	One we have known before
73.	Ẹnikúté̩	Whoever dies (young) loses respect
74.	Ẹnílọ (lóbọ̀)	The person who went away (has come back)
75.	Ẹnukónípẹ̀	The consolers are tired
76.	Ẹrunkónípẹ̀	The consolers are tired - Ìjẹ̀bú
77.	Ẹtimíríi	We have been seeing it before
78.	Ìgbẹ́kọ̀yí	The bush rejects this
79.	Igbókọ̀yí	The forest rejects this
80.	Ikúgbàyígbé	Death has forgotten this
81.	Ikúòlóògùn	No medicine to deter death; death has no medicine
82.	Ikúṣebíàlá	Death acts like a dream
83.	Ikúṣàánú	Death shows mercy (and leaves this alive)
84.	Ìlúmọ̀ọ́ká	The whole town knows its notoriety

	Name	Meaning
85.	Jáyésimi	Let the world (people) be at peace
86.	Jẹ́kíññíyì	Let me have prestige
87.	Jẹ́kíññíyìn	Let me have praise
88.	Jẹñríọgbé	Let me continue to have you to carry
89.	Jẹnsimi	Let me have rest (of mind)
90.	(A) Jítòní	He/She who wakes up today (but we are not sure of tomorrow)
91.	Jókòósẹ́nuùmi	Sit or reside in my mouth as I shall be calling you frequently, if you do not die
92.	Jókòótadé	Stay with the crown
93.	Jókòótọlá	Stay with the honour
94.	Júwò	Make it possible to be looked after
95.	Kájẹ́ró	Probably it will stay (survive)
96.	Kájọpáyé	Let us both live long on earth
97.	Kalẹ̀jayé	Sit down to enjoy life
98.	Kànnìké	The merciless, super-miser
99.	(Jẹ́) Káróunwí	Let us have something (good) to say
100.	Kárúñwí	Let us have something (good) to say
101.	Káwojúẹ̀	Let us be watching it (looking at its face)
102.	Késunko	It will not sleep in the bush
103.	Kílà	Shortened form of Kílànkó
104.	Kílànkó	What is it that is worth naming ceremoniously?
105.	Kí-ñ-níbẹ̀	What is there (that is worth noticing)?
106.	Kògbọ́dọ̀kú	Must not die
107.	Kòkúmọ́	It will not die again
108.	Kòníbiírè	He has nowhere to go (he will not die)

	Name	Meaning
109.	Kònórúkọ	It is not worth being named
110.	Kosọkọ́	There is no more hoe (to dig a grave)
111.	Kòtóyẹ (sí)	It is not worth recognising with respect
112.	Kúdáìísí	Death leaves this alone
113.	Kúùdẹ̀yìnbọ̀	Death will not come back
114.	Kúéèsàn	Death is not good (do not die)
115.	Kúfeéjì	Death forgives (and lets it survive)
116.	Kúfòmídá	Death spares me
117.	Kuforíjì	Death forgives (and lets it survive)
118.	Kújọrẹ̀	Death leaves it alone - Ìjẹ̀bù
119.	Kúkọ̀yí	Death rejects this
120.	Kúmápàyí	Death, do not kill this one
121.	Kúùnújì	Death (of it) has no shock any more
122.	Kúùnúyì	Death has no prestige (don't die)
123.	Kúsá	Death has run away
124.	Kúṣàánú	Death has mercy (has let it survive)
125.	Kúṣìímọ̀	Death makes mistakes in knowing it
126.	Kúṣòro	Death is difficult (do not try to die)
127.	Kúùtẹ̀yí	Death does not suppress this
128.	Kúyẹ̀	Death is not yet (it has changed on the child)
129.	Kúyẹ̀ba	Death changes its hiding place, and therefore will not take this child
130.	Kúyìínù	Death leaves it alone
131.	Kúyọ̀ọ́ró	Death does not kill it while killing others
132.	(Ikú) Làmbẹ̀	Death is the one we are begging
133.	Lànbẹ̀	Same as (Ikú) Làmbẹ̀

	Name	Meaning
134.	Mábadéjẹ	Do not ruin the crown
135.	Máboògùnjẹ́	Do not spoil medicine (let it be effective)
136.	Máborúkọjẹ́	Do not spoil the name (you would have been given)
137.	Mábọ̀sányìnjẹ́	Do not ridicule the deity Ọsányìn, the master herbalist
138.	Mádaríọlá	Do not change the fortune of honour
139.	Máfẹ	Do not like (death)
140.	Máfọlábọmi	Do not dip honour into water to perish
141.	Májẹ́kódùnmí	Do not let me have pain
142.	Májọ̀kùn	Do not eat millipedes (believed to be mistakenly eaten by some dead)
143.	Májọọ́lágbé	Do not let honour waste
144.	Máko (milẹ́rùlọ)	Do not deprive me of my valuables
145.	Málọmọ́	Do not go (die) again
146.	Mámòórá	Do not waste money
147.	Mámòwórá	Do not waste money
148.	Máráyésá	Do not run away from the world
149.	Mátànmí	Do not deceive me
150.	Mátẹ̀ẹ́mi	Do not ridicule me, do not make me lose respect
151.	Mátìlúkúo	Do not leave the town
152.	Mátùlúkóò	Do not leave the town - Ìjẹ̀bú
153.	Máyẹ̀n (kú)	Do not praise (death)
154.	Máyẹ̀nkú	Do not praise death
155.	Máyùn-ún-gbó	Do not go into the bush (as a corpse)
156.	Mẹ́dẹ̀yìnlọ	Do not go back (to nymph comrades)

Name	Meaning
157. Mésàákú	I cannot kill myself struggling to make it survive
158. Méyùn-ún-gbẹ́ẹ́	Do not go into the bush (as corpse)
159. Mósàákú	I cannot kill myself struggling to make it survive
160. Motúnmọrí	I see the child again
161. Mọ́kùúolú	Do not die, Olú
162. Mọ̀-yùn-úngbó	The child does not go into the forest (as corpse)
163. Ògéyíngbó	The iron deity does not praise the forest (as corpse)
164. Odùéyùn-úngbó	The Ifá corpus does not go into the forest (as corpse)
165. Ògéyùn-úngbó	The iron deity does not go into the forest (as corpse)
166. Ojútikú	Death is ashamed
167. Òkúnù	It is the dead who loses out – do not die
168. Olètúbọ̀	The thief has come back
169. Orúkọtán	All names are finished
170. Ósìnmí	It is still breathing
171. Ọjọ́yẹ̀	The day (of death) changes
172. Ọkọ́òsí	There is no hoe (to dig a grave)
173. Ọkọ́ya	The hoe has been damaged (none to dig a grave)
174. Ọmọ́bọ̀	The child has come back
175. Ọmọtúndé	The child comes again
176. Ọnikútẹ́	The one who dies loses respect
177. Pẹ́láyé	Live long

	Name	Meaning
178.	Rógbuyì	Stay to receive prestige
179.	Rósanwó	Stay to pay (back) money (spent on you)
180.	Róṣíji	Stay to (provide shadow) protect your parents
181.	Rótìlú	Stay with the town
182.	Rótìmí	Stay with me
183.	Rótọlá	Stay with honour
184.	Rówàyé	Stay to look at the world, and enjoy life
185.	(U) Rúnṣèwé	Nothing happens to this (this will survive) - Ìjẹ̀bú
186.	Ṣeéwò	Be possible to be looked after (to be nurtured)
187.	Ṣekóoní	Work hard to grow up, and possess something
188.	Ṣẹ̀wọ́níkú	Stop dying again and again
189.	Ṣẹ̀wọ́núkú	Stop dying again and again - Ìjẹ̀bú
190.	Ṣíwọ́okú	Stop dying again and again
191.	Tanímọ́ọ̀wò	Who really knows how to take care of this?
192.	Táwojú	The one we are watching (looking at its face)
193.	Tijúikú	Be ashamed to die
194.	Tòrudàgbà	Child who is always healthy during the night but behaves deadly ill during the day, every day
195.	Tugbóbọ̀	Comes back from the bush/forest (reincarnated from its last grave)
196.	Yémiítàn	Stop deceiving me (that you will survive)

About The Author

Dr. Báyọ̀ Odùṣínà is an International Management Consultant.

For many years in the 60's and 70's, he was a classroom teacher of Yorùbá language and culture in Secondary Schools and Teacher Training Colleges in Nigeria. He taught Yorùbá language to some students of Newton High School, Mass,. U.S.A. in 1970.

His other works in Yorùbá literature include Bánúsọ, Òpìtàn Ṣékélé, Ìbon Ìléwọ́ and "Eréùn Ìjẹ̀bú Yún" a book written in Ìjẹ̀bú "language".

Table of Index

Èkìtì 43, 45, 56
Ìjẹ̀bús 19
abode 44, 52
achieve 22
acquire 52
affluence 25, 90
aggressive 59, 127, 139, 141
Aláàfin 18, 91, 94, 128, 141
alive 26, 50, 67, 152, 154, 155
ancestry 18, 19, 48, 137, 143
annoy 120
annoyed 23, 92, 128
anxiety 97, 106, 115
anxious 69, 117
appeases 23, 26, 27, 54
appreciate 41, 54
Arabic 131
armours 28
army 24, 28, 54, 55, 97, 112, 128, 134
arrive .. 32, 45, 47, 60, 64, 65, 87, 89, 93, 95, 96, 100, 103, 108, 109, 113, 114, 115, 116, 117, 119, 121, 147, 149
arrives . 15, 18, 24, 25, 26, 27, 28, 32, 33, 37, 38, 40, 42, 51, 56, 58, 66, 73, 81, 124, 152
ashamed 57, 71, 140, 159, 160
asked 49, 60, 149, 150
assemble 49, 116
assembles . 22, 23, 24, 25, 26, 38, 39, 40, 41, 50, 56, 71, 75, 76, 95, 106
assure 40
attention 31, 34, 127
authority 27, 42, 124
avenge 35, 128
awe 27, 46
awesome 29, 43
back 1, 22, 24, 25, 26, 27, 30, 31, 32, 33, 34, 35, 37, 38, 47, 52, 53, 55, 56, 57, 59, 62, 63, 66, 69, 74, 75, 79, 80, 84, 85, 86, 89, 92, 95, 102, 105, 111, 118, 154, 155, 157, 158, 159, 160

banana 129
barn 131
barrenness 28, 53
bathe 48
beach 138
bead 37, 43, 124, 141
beads 6, 19, 35, 38, 42, 147, 148
beautiful 75, 90, 126, 127, 136, 137, 147, 148, 151
beauty 23, 70, 147
befits ... 23, 26, 61, 62, 63, 67, 68, 70, 73, 75, 78, 79, 116
beg 6, 9, 23, 49, 112
Beg 134, 146
behind 41, 50
belong 49, 108, 125, 138
benefactor 105, 108, 123
benefits 52, 53, 62, 68, 117
benevolence 53
binds 27, 67, 150
bird 132
birth-weight 98
black 37, 90, 99, 114, 127, 147
blacksmith 37, 93, 113, 114, 128, 130, 132, 140, 155
blacksmiths 19, 93
blemish 29
blessing 28, 35, 36, 54, 100, 103
block 28, 53, 129, 131, 136
blocks 28, 127
bluff 48, 58, 134, 135
bluffs 32, 77, 94, 146
boat 127
bold 40
brass 20, 97, 136
brass smiths 20
brave 9, 10, 18, 28, 30, 33, 42, 44, 50, 61, 63, 71, 80, 104, 111, 133, 144
breathe 23, 30, 32, 45, 58, 91
breed 43, 140, 147

bring ... 30, 33, 34, 40, 41, 44, 45, 46, 47, 55, 62, 71, 72, 92, 113, 127, 133
build 22, 23, 28, 41, 46, 95, 126
building 73
bush 59, 152, 155, 156, 158, 159, 160
business 73
calabash 34, 134
called 9, 21, 25, 49, 90, 128, 146, 149
camwood 8, 9, 46
captive 36
captures 32
carefulness 31
catch 42, 43, 134
celebrate 134
chair 22, 52, 131
chalk 18, 40, 45
changes 56, 62, 65, 157, 159
character 70, 106
charcoal 99
chase 43
chastise 23
cheat 37
chieftaincy .. 2, 19, 24, 25, 27, 29, 32, 33, 35, 37, 38, 39, 40, 42, 44, 45, 46, 48, 49, 50, 51, 52, 53, 56, 57, 58, 60, 61, 62, 67, 70, 73, 74, 76, 88, 89, 93, 97, 99, 103, 105, 107, 114, 117, 118, 124, 126, 128, 129, 130, 131, 132, 133, 134, 135, 136, 137, 138, 140, 141, 142, 143, 144, 153, 155
Chieftaincy 20, 107, 118
child 14, 75, 76, 77, 78, 81, 82, 83, 84, 85, 86, 88, 89, 92, 93, 94, 95, 96, 97, 98, 99, 100, 101, 102, 103, 104, 105, 106, 107, 108, 109, 110, 111, 112, 113, 114, 115, 116, 117, 118, 119, 120, 121, 122, 123, 124, 125, 144, 152, 160
children 2, 7, 9, 10, 18, 19, 20, 21, 25, 37, 39, 40, 43, 48, 63, 83, 84, 86, 87, 92, 95, 98, 99, 100, 101, 103, 106, 107, 111, 116, 118, 121, 123, 135, 150, 152
chip 53, 136
chosen 59
circle 92
clean 48
cleave 52
clothweavers 20
coconut 139
cold 19, 84, 127, 130
collect 38, 40, 41, 52, 130, 135, 141
collides 27, 127
combines 40, 60, 68
comfort 59, 106
commerce 7, 73, 114, 143
compensates ... 28, 31, 33, 41, 44, 52, 54, 68
compensation 30, 102, 107, 109
complain 51
complete . 1, 7, 24, 28, 29, 31, 32, 33, 36, 39, 44, 45, 49, 50, 53, 55, 56, 61, 71, 75, 82, 111, 113, 121, 132, 133, 142, 149
comrade 61, 101, 119, 127, 132, 134, 158
conflict .. 8, 9, 34, 61, 100, 101, 104, 117, 120, 122
confront 140
congregation 27
conquer 54, 72, 145
consolation 28, 36, 106
consolatory 50
console 35, 50, 55, 72, 100, 155
conspiracy 32, 58
coral 6, 19, 35, 38, 42, 45, 48, 57, 76, 147
courage 40, 47, 121, 133
courageous 42
coward 139, 153, 154
cradle 150
craftmanship 31
craftsmanship 20, 25, 45, 46

163

Craftsmanship 20
cries 44, 81, 85, 95
crime.. 123
crowd................................... 48, 60, 89
crown 8, 9, 22, 24, 25, 26, 27, 30, 31, 32, 33, 34, 35, 36, 40, 41, 44, 45, 48, 50, 51, 52, 53, 54, 55, 56, 57, 58, 62, 67, 70, 75, 76, 87, 89, 90, 93, 97, 99, 102, 103, 106, 110, 111, 112, 116, 123, 128, 131, 134, 135, 138, 151, 154, 156, 158
Crown 18
cruelty.. 48, 54
crystal 9, 58
cult............ 16, 18, 19, 20, 23, 88, 95, 96
cultured.. 144
cure 19, 150
curfews 19, 20
cutlass.. 132
dainty 126, 150
dance 38, 91
dancing 30, 96, 127
danger 29
deaf.. 41
death 9, 10, 15, 43, 52, 69, 71, 81, 82, 84, 86, 90, 97, 102, 104, 105, 107, 108, 116, 133, 155, 157, 158, 159
deceive 30, 49, 54, 87, 158
deity.. 8, 9, 10, 20, 24, 26, 30, 46, 58, 74, 81, 87, 102, 114, 115, 120, 124, 128, 130, 140, 141, 158, 159
delicate 45, 48, 65, 109, 147
deserve 48
detractor.. 109
die 41, 84, 86, 96, 98, 104, 107, 108, 109, 112, 124, 125
dies 66, 81, 82, 153, 155, 159
difficult 43, 88, 157
diginity 73
dignify 30, 44, 47, 48, 59, 69, 90, 91, 127, 134, 138, 142

dignity . 23, 33, 35, 40, 43, 47, 54, 56, 68, 72, 78, 80, 91, 94, 101, 104, 105, 106, 128, 132, 134, 143, 153
dilute 42
diminished 50
disappointment 98, 105
disperses 32
divination . 8, 9, 20, 46, 74, 82, 83, 84, 85
divinity 14, 18, 19, 20, 21, 23, 24, 26, 39, 43, 47, 61, 89, 104, 110, 112, 113, 117, 121
dog 129, 152
domestic 43
dove... 148
dreadlocks.. 82
drum 22, 38, 44, 54, 89, 116, 120
drum sticks.. 22
drummers 18, 20, 95
drums.................................... 20, 26, 44
dunghill 152
ears 43
easy. 2, 27, 35, 37, 45, 50, 52, 54, 60, 73, 91, 95, 98, 117, 123, 135, 139
education 2, 12, 30
efficacious 15, 46, 67, 98, 117
eight 27
Ekìtì 55
elders 16, 45, 133, 144
Elephant.. 18
elite... 123
emerge 40, 41, 62, 119
encirclement 52
encourage 45
end 5, 36, 48, 77, 137
endowments 19
enemy 27, 28, 50, 54, 72, 144
enough 31, 39, 43, 46, 51, 57, 58, 59, 60, 61, 66, 72, 75, 77, 96, 97, 99, 100, 124, 127, 133, 135, 136, 151
envy 44, 46, 120
errand 50

espouses 30
European 4, 23, 58
evening 22, 96
evil 18, 19, 22, 28, 36, 71, 117
excel 34, 46, 50, 62, 78, 149
exhibits 31, 78, 92
exonerates 60
expanse 27, 29, 41
exterminated 52, 108
eye 71, 113, 147, 153
eyes 54, 82, 123, 138
fade 49
faint 84
fame 33, 44, 49, 56, 61, 65, 147
family .. 1, 2, 9, 10, 12, 14, 16, 17, 18, 19, 20, 23, 26, 28, 29, 31, 34, 39, 40, 42, 48, 49, 55, 56, 57, 60, 61, 76, 79, 80, 87, 88, 89, 90, 93, 94, 95, 96, 97, 98, 99, 100, 101, 102, 103, 104, 105, 106, 107, 108, 109, 110, 111, 112, 113, 114, 115, 116, 117, 118, 119, 120, 121, 122, 123, 124, 125, 126, 128, 130, 136, 138, 141, 143, 151
famine 28, 36, 71, 106
famous 36, 37, 39, 41, 43, 47, 48, 92, 114, 119
farm 63, 64, 92, 100, 114, 127, 130, 132, 133, 136, 141
fashionable 45, 138
fate 19, 20, 116, 117, 121
Fate 19
father .. 14, 23, 35, 38, 57, 66, 81, 82, 85, 88, 89, 90, 91, 93, 94, 97, 98, 99, 101, 102, 103, 105, 106, 107, 108, 109, 110, 112, 113, 114, 117, 118, 119, 120, 121, 123, 124, 133, 137
favour 48, 57, 110
fear 27, 36, 45, 128, 132, 139
feared 57, 92, 140

female . 14, 15, 16, 18, 23, 38, 41, 83, 84, 92, 93, 94, 101, 106, 110, 111, 116, 118, 136, 144, 148
festival 18, 24, 25, 31, 44, 46, 58, 81, 85, 87, 88, 89, 95, 96, 110, 113, 114, 119, 144
fight 6, 31, 32, 33, 36, 41, 53, 88, 93, 100, 116, 117, 119, 126, 127, 136, 140, 149
filth 43
find 50, 51, 52, 59, 97, 134, 135, 150
fingers 84
finish . 25, 26, 36, 39, 41, 55, 56, 75, 112, 123, 159
flatter 50
flock 92
flourish 50
flows 19, 53
flutter 60
forest 29, 30, 35, 68, 155, 159, 160
forget 12, 33, 34, 35, 36, 44
forgets 48
forgive 38, 157
fort 28
fraudulent 54
free 61, 74, 104
friend 74, 120, 132, 144
friendship 79
fright 8, 9, 36, 42, 45, 46
frightens 22
functional 26
future .. 1, 37, 44, 76, 100, 111, 112, 119, 143
generous 35, 107, 126, 133
gestation 85
gift .. 26, 46, 48, 56, 66, 89, 100, 101, 122
gives .. 2, 8, 10, 14, 22, 23, 24, 25, 26, 31, 32, 37, 38, 39, 40, 43, 47, 54, 55, 56, 58, 60, 61, 63, 66, 67, 72, 75, 78, 96, 97, 100, 104, 120, 128, 131, 133, 138
gloat 39, 98, 102, 109

165

God ... 8, 9, 19, 31, 44, 68, 72, 75, 81, 87, 88, 91, 99, 100, 103, 104, 105, 106, 110, 111, 112, 115, 116, 120, 121, 122, 124, 125, 142, 144, 145, 153, 154
gold 56, 125
goldsmith 138
goldsmiths 20
good.. 8, 9, 18, 22, 24, 26, 28, 31, 32, 33, 36, 40, 41, 43, 47, 51, 52, 53, 54, 56, 58, 59, 60, 62, 63, 67, 68, 69, 70, 75, 76, 77, 79, 92, 100, 106, 118, 120, 121, 124, 126, 127, 130, 135, 141, 152, 156, 157
goodness.. 23
graduation 25, 105, 118
grandfather........81, 82, 94, 97, 100, 101, 106, 108, 110, 112, 117
grapevine... 109
grateful 32, 46, 53, 99, 123, 124
gratitude 29, 42, 79, 122
grave 152, 157, 159, 160
great 31, 74, 96, 105, 112, 118, 125
guard 60
guest 134
guilty 37, 95
hammer 114
handsome 89, 99, 126, 137, 140, 151
happiness... 40
hardship... 48
harmattan.. 127
hawk 15, 136, 153
head.... 15, 19, 20, 23, 27, 58, 62, 77, 81, 82, 91, 107, 116, 117, 127, 128, 137, 144
health.. 24, 95
healthy.................37, 52, 59, 91, 93, 160
hears 36, 53, 98, 128
heaven 15, 19, 137, 154
heir . 16, 37, 90, 107, 114, 134, 137, 140, 143

herb 18, 67, 125, 127, 131, 140, 158
herbs................................ 15, 19, 34, 125
hereditary 28
hides 30
highway 123
history..............25, 28, 50, 101, 102, 119
hoe 130, 157, 159
holy 89, 94
home..... 1, 14, 22, 25, 26, 27, 32, 34, 35, 43, 47, 49, 50, 51, 53, 56, 57, 59, 60, 62, 63, 64, 65, 71, 74, 75, 77, 80, 84, 89, 90, 93, 99, 105, 111, 113, 114, 115, 123, 127, 132, 138
honest.. 43
honey 29, 40, 73, 74, 110, 118, 148
honour .. 9, 10, 14, 22, 23, 25, 26, 27, 29, 30, 31, 32, 33, 34, 35, 36, 37, 38, 39, 40, 41, 42, 43, 44, 46, 48, 49, 50, 51, 52, 53, 54, 55, 57, 58, 60, 62, 63, 65, 66, 68, 70, 71, 72, 73, 74, 75, 77, 78, 79, 80, 88, 89, 90, 91, 92, 94, 96, 97, 98, 99, 100, 101, 102, 103, 104, 105, 106, 107, 108, 109, 110, 111, 112, 113, 116, 117, 118, 119, 120, 121, 122, 123, 124, 125, 126, 130, 131, 134, 135, 137, 141, 146, 148, 150, 151, 154, 156, 158, 160
honourable 37, 57, 89, 121
honours........................ 26, 62, 100, 113
hope................................. 104, 105, 106
horse.. 23, 43
horseback 103
hostilities 53
house 7, 23, 24, 26, 27, 28, 30, 39, 40, 41, 44, 47, 49, 50, 51, 55, 59, 60, 61, 64, 65, 69, 73, 74, 75, 78, 90, 96, 102, 105, 107, 116, 118, 126, 129, 134, 135, 136, 137, 138, 148, 154
human.. 29
humble... 30
hundred 14, 27, 29, 49

166

hunter 20, 25, 42, 46, 89, 131, 143
hunters 19, 20
hurry 51, 109
hyperactive 126
Ifá 19, 20, 22, 24, 28, 46
Ìjẹ̀bú 24, 26, 28, 31, 32, 33, 38, 42, 43, 47, 49
ill treatment 28, 41
imagination 44
immigrants 20
important 7, 39, 54, 76, 101, 119, 134, 136, 137
impossible 42, 102
incorrigible 126
increase 26, 29, 43, 45, 50, 59, 65
indebted 47
indigo 135, 136, 137
inexhaustible 89
infertility 95
inspection 47
insult 26, 64, 118
investment 64, 93, 129
iron 8, 9, 10, 14, 19, 24, 37, 42, 110, 112, 113, 128, 130, 132, 140, 159
island 29
jealous 38, 118
jealousy 46
jester 138
joker 144
journey 22, 29, 56, 58, 66, 80, 81, 88
joy . 14, 23, 26, 27, 28, 29, 31, 32, 37, 40, 42, 44, 53, 58, 60, 63, 65, 68, 72, 73, 77, 80, 100, 101, 105, 107, 111, 112, 115, 118, 123, 124
joyful 44, 46, 56, 59, 66, 76
joyous 58, 62, 77, 96, 105, 111, 112, 113, 134, 144, 147
justifies 8, 9, 27, 72
kills 65, 69, 142, 143
kind 54, 120
kindness 55, 60, 112, 122

king . 7, 10, 20, 24, 25, 26, 58, 62, 77, 80, 92, 107, 109, 110, 111, 112, 114, 118, 120, 124, 128, 131, 132, 133, 134, 135, 136, 137, 140, 141, 142, 143, 144, 154
knowledge 39, 48, 51, 105
knows 4, 5, 44, 45, 46, 51, 66, 67, 70, 95, 101, 116, 117, 120, 124, 142, 145, 155, 160
labour ... 83, 84, 88, 91, 93, 95, 112, 115, 117, 123, 130
lament 26
lamp 52
landlord 114, 142
lazy 43
lead 13, 43, 140, 141
leak 44
learning 30
leave 41, 50, 91, 158
lick 46
life . 42, 47, 56, 60, 65, 82, 91, 93, 96, 97, 98, 101, 102, 106, 107, 109, 110, 111, 112, 118, 124, 129, 130, 137, 143, 153, 154, 155, 156
light 23, 52, 100, 127, 138
lightning 21
liked 61, 78
lineage 40
listen 109
listens 27, 37, 43, 57
live 46, 51, 63, 89, 129, 135, 153, 155, 156
lose 10, 37, 48, 53, 56, 136, 154, 158
loud 6, 7, 44, 94, 131
love 7, 14, 32, 68, 100, 101, 103, 115, 146
loves 30, 31, 32, 66, 72, 75, 115, 121
luck 43, 47, 60, 141
magnanimity 33
march 40

167

mark.. 6, 8, 9, 10, 11, 42, 44, 47, 52, 104, 115
market 29
masquerade 18, 82, 87, 90, 128, 138
mat 57
measure 47
mechanics 19
medicine ... 46, 58, 67, 84, 100, 116, 117, 132, 139, 145, 152, 155, 158
memory 8, 9, 41, 42, 43, 49
menstruate 83
merchant 133, 145
mercy 53, 87, 155, 157
merits 38
messenger 18, 104
middle 4, 7, 11, 87, 96
migrated 18
millipede 158
mind 8, 9, 48, 51, 56, 66, 153, 156
miserly 126
misfortune 40, 98, 102, 109, 113
mix 23, 26, 27, 29, 31, 32, 35, 40, 44, 45, 46, 50, 62, 68, 73, 79
molar 100
money ... 7, 10, 12, 14, 16, 31, 47, 48, 52, 55, 64, 73, 75, 78, 85, 93, 102, 107, 117, 118, 122, 128, 129, 132, 133, 134, 135, 136, 138, 139, 142, 143, 150, 151, 152, 158, 160
moon 29, 31, 132
morning 16, 37, 38, 58, 93, 110, 130, 142, 149, 152
mother 14, 24, 37, 38, 74, 79, 81, 83, 84, 85, 86, 91, 92, 93, 96, 97, 100, 101, 106, 112, 115, 119, 120, 121, 124, 125, 153
mountain 57, 136, 141
Mountain 19
mouth 139, 156
needle-workers 20
new 16, 26, 29, 31, 50, 124, 132

night 22, 23, 81, 84, 85, 160
noble 28
nurture 47
obey 103
ocean .. 24, 25, 28, 38, 40, 42, 49, 57, 74, 115
oil 155
olú 28, 50, 53, 87, 103, 122, 141, 159
Ondo 18, 20
opens 41, 42, 54, 55, 72, 74, 123
opponent 129
ornamentation 20, 23, 25, 26, 35, 45, 147
Orò 19, 20
outlives 27
overwhelms 24, 107
Oǹdó .. 28, 32, 41, 42, 49, 50, 51, 96, 144
packages 28
pain 37, 51, 71, 158
palace . 24, 26, 27, 37, 41, 48, 49, 59, 60, 62, 68, 89, 103, 125, 143
palm-tree 20
pamper 16, 31, 32, 34, 37, 42, 48, 51, 52, 61, 66, 75, 76, 90, 93, 97, 104, 107, 110, 116, 130, 131, 146, 147, 150, 155
pampers 23, 30, 31, 32, 38, 39, 40, 50, 72
paramount 19, 24, 28, 33, 87, 90, 94, 103, 104, 115, 123, 125, 134, 135
parent 37, 40, 93, 121, 125
parenthood 8, 9, 29, 121, 122, 125
peaceful 59, 139, 148
peacefully 53
pedigree .. 31, 38, 41, 52, 60, 61, 78, 103, 115, 142, 153
Pedigree 18, 19, 103
people 1, 2, 9, 10, 16, 21, 28, 30
perfect 26, 38, 43, 44, 91
perfection 26, 130

pet-name 1, 93, 127, 128, 129, 131, 133, 134, 136, 137, 139, 140, 142
piggy-back 31, 92
pillar 27, 151
pity 60
plain 56
plead 6, 9, 10, 23, 34, 35, 49
pleases 29, 60, 61, 64
plebeian 112
popular 40, 46, 133, 138, 139, 144
position 25, 27, 62, 74
positive 10, 40, 41, 51
possess 30, 49, 53, 97, 111, 146, 149, 150
posterity ... 39, 41, 47, 51, 56, 59, 65, 76, 102, 119
potent 48
poverty 122
power 46, 116, 117, 129, 132
powerful 21, 56, 57, 58, 59, 109, 116, 133, 136, 145
praise 29, 34, 36, 46, 54, 61, 78, 103, 120, 137, 150, 156, 158, 159
praised 31, 36, 39, 58, 59, 62, 75
prayers 90, 106
precious .. 58, 78, 91, 103, 107, 112, 118, 122, 148, 149
prestige 26, 29, 30, 34, 36, 37, 39, 45, 47, 48, 51, 58, 59, 61, 63, 64, 69, 70, 72, 74, 77, 92, 106, 108, 116, 151, 156, 157, 160
prestigious .. 36, 58, 61, 69, 92, 107, 112, 113, 116
pride 30, 46, 48
primogenitor 120
profit 27
profitable 29, 34, 64, 68, 93, 129
Profitable 93
progress 49
prominent .. 118, 124, 131, 133, 141, 152
promise 33, 35, 38, 53, 54, 105

prosperity 37
prosperous 9, 10, 37, 42, 63, 133, 135
prospers 61
protection 28, 49, 52, 59, 77, 91, 103, 110
protective 48, 78, 116
protects 31, 49, 54, 55
publicize 40, 56
punishment 28, 60, 107, 111, 112, 126
quarrel .. 7, 14, 30, 31, 35, 42, 68, 87, 88, 89, 95, 101, 102, 104, 140
quickly 54, 84
rain 15, 23, 24, 44, 87, 96, 128, 135, 136, 139
ravage 26
reach 45, 49, 52, 53, 62, 91, 101
reason 48
rebellion 26, 32, 42, 54, 80, 123, 124, 127
recede 24
recognized 49, 84, 141
refuge 52, 112
regret 38
re-incarnated 18
reincarnation 82, 115
rejoice 62, 67, 70, 115, 142
relatives 14, 29, 30, 45, 76, 77, 88, 90, 94, 109, 115, 121, 130, 132, 134, 136, 144
relief 37, 97, 113
remain 40, 41, 44, 55, 56, 57, 105, 123
remaining 41
remember 50
remould 64
repairs 55, 56, 59
replacement 52, 54
reply 45
reproach 43, 47, 48
respect .. 4, 16, 37, 38, 44, 47, 48, 56, 62, 68, 123, 153, 154, 155, 157, 158, 159
responds 27

169

response 43
restored 25
rich .. 23, 27, 36, 56, 90, 92, 98, 102, 104, 114, 123, 126, 128, 132, 133, 138, 141, 142, 143, 151
ridicule ... 36, 44, 57, 87, 90, 98, 105, 158
river 10, 14, 19, 21, 49, 89, 95, 115, 127, 131, 139
road ... 26, 33, 42, 50, 55, 58, 60, 95, 116
roadside 88, 140
rock 133, 150
rotund 147
row 43
runs 52, 66, 95, 118, 127
Sabbath 46, 81, 94
sacrifice 43, 82, 85, 117, 138, 140
sad 15, 45, 109
sadness 15, 35, 43, 59, 108, 118
safe 41, 42, 62, 117, 122, 124
salt 40
salvation 8, 9, 33, 34, 36, 43, 51
Sàngó 21, 22
save 8, 9, 12, 34, 35, 38, 62, 75, 126
saviour 58
scarce 9, 10, 36, 55, 61, 77, 78
scold 23
scramble 43, 90, 104, 109, 129, 146
sea 25, 113, 115
search 42, 60, 82, 83, 98, 101, 153
searches 60
select 43, 58, 147
settle 47, 50, 59, 129, 149, 154
settlement 28, 32, 100, 142, 149
shade 48
shame 28
sharp 47, 67
shoe 137
shrine 121
shy 122
silver 138
sleep 53, 91

small 94, 95, 131
small pox 20, 25, 118
social status 19, 76, 102, 118
spy 136
stamina 32, 43, 45
starve 52
stays 22, 23, 24, 25, 26, 34, 51, 52, 56, 57, 72, 113
steadfast 135
steal 36, 37, 38
stigma 60
storm 8, 9, 36
strength 28, 32, 40
strike 53
strong 33, 38, 40, 47, 128, 136
struggle 153, 159
stud 140
succeeds 24
successor 90
suffer 38, 109
superior 30, 39, 45, 54, 55, 75
supplication 34, 106
support 27, 30, 32, 34, 35, 40, 44, 51, 52, 57, 59, 67, 80, 99, 103, 115, 119, 120, 121, 134, 135, 136
supports 24, 25, 28
supreme 20, 22, 33, 42, 43, 44, 52, 55, 125, 133
surround 62, 65
survive 23, 34, 59, 91, 97, 103, 136, 153, 155, 156, 157, 159, 160
survives 29, 30, 31, 34, 41, 42, 45, 61, 76, 77
survivor 24
sustain 36, 46, 47, 61
swallow 46
sweet 29, 46, 59, 65, 67, 73, 75, 76, 103, 130, 153, 155
swims 60
sword 54
tailors 20

170

tall 33, 127, 128, 132, 138, 140, 151
tears 15, 51
thank 110
thanks 29, 48, 63, 79, 111, 122, 123, 124
thoughtful 8, 9, 31, 48
throne 33, 35, 40, 44, 46, 48, 49, 50, 106, 128, 150
thunder 21, 133, 153
timber 133
tired 53, 145, 155
toes 83, 84
tomorrow 46, 65, 101, 124, 145, 152, 156
tooth 138, 147
totem .. 12, 14, 18, 19, 20, 21, 26, 39, 88, 91, 93, 94, 95, 107, 122, 124, 130
touch 23, 30, 32, 39
tough 22, 95, 128, 131
town ... 26, 27, 30, 35, 36, 39, 40, 42, 52, 54, 56, 57, 59, 60, 61, 62, 67, 70, 71, 80, 95, 96, 99, 101, 103, 109, 117, 137, 140, 142, 143, 144, 154, 155, 158, 160
trial 47, 51
tribal marks 127
triplets 83
triumph 116
trouble 48, 98
truth 55, 117
twin 83
twins 15, 23, 81, 83, 84, 86
two 14, 27, 28, 29, 39, 49, 65, 77, 86, 92, 93, 104, 106, 107, 115
umbilical cord .. 15, 49, 81, 83, 84, 85, 86
umbrella 96
uncomplicated 91, 95
unconquerable 29, 117, 126
unfortunate 62
untouchable 126
upright 33, 56, 128, 134, 140, 149
valuable 45, 56, 73, 76, 77, 97, 103

velvet 127, 131, 135, 143, 147
vengeance 67, 102
vindicate 36, 103, 117
visit 23, 55, 60, 61, 62, 136
vocation 104, 120
voice 46, 126, 131, 132
wakes .. 23, 25, 37, 38, 53, 59, 67, 74, 75, 82, 93, 94, 129, 130, 140, 152, 153, 156
walk 25, 31, 32, 33, 38, 46, 51, 55, 82, 89, 90, 91, 126
wall 46, 126, 139
war 24, 26, 36, 41, 42, 51, 54, 57, 80, 88, 89, 93, 104, 112, 119, 124, 127, 133, 134, 136
War 71, 80, 132
warfare 23, 43, 104
warrior 18, 21, 22, 61, 104, 113, 114, 127, 133, 134, 141
warriors 9, 10, 20, 142, 144
waste 40, 47, 158
water. 6, 8, 14, 19, 27, 29, 32, 49, 81, 82, 84, 85, 115, 117, 126, 158
Water 19
weaken 49
wealth . 22, 23, 25, 28, 29, 35, 37, 41, 44, 46, 47, 49, 52, 53, 55, 60, 61, 63, 73, 76, 88, 90, 94, 95, 98, 107, 114, 121, 133, 135, 136, 138, 141, 143
wealthy . 34, 35, 45, 56, 59, 92, 107, 121, 130, 131, 133, 144, 149
weeping 23, 27, 28, 35, 56, 61
welfare 54
white 30, 40, 45, 86, 87, 95, 99, 150
wicked 69
wins 24, 54
wisdom 20, 35, 55, 98, 137
wise .. 35, 39, 45, 48, 56, 75, 95, 129, 132
wizard 20, 95, 107
wolf 129
womb 34, 50

171

wonders 26, 41, 50
wood carvers 20
world 9, 10, 15, 24, 30, 47, 65, 77, 92, 95, 96, 98, 107, 109, 129, 137, 153, 154, 155, 156, 158, 160
worship 12, 18, 19, 26, 28, 29, 35, 36, 37, 42, 46, 58, 59, 61, 81, 88, 89, 94, 112, 128, 129, 141

worshipper 20, 25, 51, 94, 113, 114, 115, 121, 128, 130, 142
worthy 25, 38, 39, 44, 49, 53, 56, 57, 58, 59, 76, 100, 135
yams 133
year 15, 87, 89, 118, 119